Ancient Asian History

A Captivating Guide to the Ancient Civilizations of China and Japan

Free Bonus from Captivating History
(Available for a Limited time)

Hi History Lovers!

Now you have a chance to join our exclusive history list so you can get your first history ebook for free as well as discounts and a potential to get more history books for free! Simply visit the link below to join.

Captivatinghistory.com/ebook

Also, make sure to follow us on Facebook, Twitter and Youtube by searching for Captivating History.

Contents

Part 1: Ancient China

A Captivating Guide to the Ancient History of China and the Chinese Civilization Starting from the Shang Dynasty to the Fall of the Han Dynasty

Introduction

China today is a country of many controversies. Its industry is booming, but it's a socialist state. The communist party is the undisputed ruler of the entire nation, with many Orwellian features in its dictatorship. Even Chinese society seems to be rather collectivistic in nature. With the centralized economy, a strong people's army, and a clear leftist ideology, China today is without a doubt a communist country, which, unlike most of its predecessors, seems to be functioning and here to stay. But despite all that, there is a resemblance between this modern People's Republic and Imperial China of the past, as the same blood of the red dragon flows through its veins. And though ideology has changed quite substantially, it looks like the philosophy behind it remained the same. So, to understand present-day China, its politics, society, and culture in general, we have to go back to the beginnings of the Chinese civilization.

It was during this early period that the Chinese people emerged from a local power to one of the most important states in the world, developing its own worldviews, philosophy of life and politics, and creating a civilization to last millennia to come. And no matter how much time has passed, and the influence that came through time, these roots remain deeply embedded in Chinese society. The best examples of this are the thoughts of Confucius as well as the writings of Sun Tzu, both of whom lived in during the period of ancient China; these two figures are probably the most well-known Chinese in the world, rivaled only by the infamous chairman Mao. But even if you are not curious about understanding how China came to be today, you should be interested in Chinese history, as some of the world's greatest achievements in science, technology, philosophy, and art came from its civilization. Its contribution to the cultural heritage of the human race is enormous; one may even argue the most important. Yet due to misunderstandings and current political climate, Western audiences often overlook it. And that is a mistake that should not be made.

And this guide is a good first step in avoiding that mistake. You will be led on a journey through almost 2,000 years of Chinese history, showing you all the ups and downs of those ancient times, the sufferings and joys of the Chinese people, along with their greatest achievements and failures. Dynasties will change, people will be killed and born, art made and destroyed, but the Chinese civilization will prevail, rising from humble beginnings to an empire that at some points outshined any other in the world at that time. And yet it won't be only a tale of kings and queens, emperors and rulers, of palaces and forts, or of swords and shields. It will also tell a story of farmers and merchants, artisans and artists, philosophers and scientists. And hopefully by the end of this introductory guide, you will gain a sense of what, who, and how the Chinese civilization was made as great as it was and still is. From that, a better understanding of this amazing Far Eastern culture and its history should arise as well as a greater appreciation of its achievements and contributions to the world. And with a better knowledge of history, a clearer understanding of the world will come as well.

Chapter 1 – Chinese Lands and Birth of China

A long, long time ago, a giant god named Pangu had awoken from a prolonged slumber in a chaotic egg-like shaped universe, finding only darkness around him. Unsatisfied, he used his ax to split the egg into two pieces creating the earth (black Yin) and the sky (white Yang). And after eighteen thousand years of loneliness, he died, leaving his body to decay and transform into mountains, rivers, forests, and other geological and botanical features. In one version, he created humans from clay before he died because he felt the universe was too empty, while in another they came from the fleas that lived on Pangu's fur, which were spread across the earth by the wind when he died. This is one of the old Chinese creation myths of both the universe and the human race, or to be more precise, the Chinese people. For centuries this was one of the stories in which the ancient Chinese believed in, but of course today, we know better than to look at the legends as the truth.

1. Illustration of giant god Pangu. Source: https://commons.wikimedia.org

Archeological facts give us a completely different story of the early settlement of China, which maybe isn't as imaginative or fun, but is by no mean less impressive. The oldest fossil remains found in China date around 2 million years ago. These remains are from Homo Erectus, the predecessor of Homo Sapiens, or modern man. This means that China was settled from the Early Stone Age, scientifically known as the Paleolithic Era. These pre-humans, as we might call the Homo Erectus, settled across large areas of what is modern China, and show rather significant diversity in their tool usage and way of life. Around 300,000 years ago, these pre-humans started to evolve into Homo Sapiens both in Africa, the cradle of humankind, as well as in Asia. Some of the earliest settlements of modern man in China dates from around 200-250,000 years ago, and from that time, development of tools and social life started to speed up until it culminated in what is today called the "Neolithic (New Stone Age) Revolution" that started somewhere between 8-10,000 years ago. In that period, agriculture developed in China, like in the other "cradles of civilization." The main crops of these Neolithic settlements were rice and millet. They also started to show signs of more complicated tools, like spears, arrows, hooks, and needles, as well as the first signs of rituals. These early cultures also domesticated dogs and pigs, and in later periods started making crude ceramics. Of course, it is too early to mark these early humans as the Chinese people, but they were most likely their ancestors.

The main area of the early settlements of the Chinese ancestors was around the Yellow (Huang) River and its largest tributary, Wei River, which lay south of present-day Beijing. Later on, they spread farther south to another major river in China, the Yangtze River, which is also the longest river in Asia. These areas weren't chosen randomly, but thanks to the flooding and the fertilizing materials they brought from the plains on the east, they made a rather fertile land on their banks. That made them rather attractive for the early humans as they made farming much easier with their primitive tools. Another important detail is the fact that roughly in the middle between the Yellow and Yangtze Rivers draws the line where rice cultivation stops due to the change in the climate. The warmer and rainier weather to the south of that line allows for rice to be grown, and also makes southern China more tropical, with dense jungles and heavy rainfalls. On the north, millet was the main crop as the climate is more continental, with mild and warm summers and rather cold winters. And also, there is much less rain in northern China. It is also worth noting that the area between these two major rivers is mostly flat, with mountains growing taller as you head west. On the northwestern borders of these plains lies a dry steppe which eventually turns into a desert today known as the Gobi, near the modern Chinese-Mongolian border. In the east and south lies the Yellow Sea and the Pacific Ocean, in which both of the aforementioned rivers flow into.

Even from the basic geography, two things become obvious rather quickly. First, the land between the Yellow and Yangtze Rivers is rather fertile and suitable for settlement. That is apparent from the fact that even today the most densely populated area of China is the region between those rivers. The other is that the lands of the early Chinese were surrounded by natural obstacles: thick jungles to the south, high mountains to the west, dry deserts to the north, and a vast ocean to the east. This allowed the early Chinese society to grow separately from the other people and cultures that were around them, allowing for a rather unique and specific development of the Chinese civilization. By the early 3rd millennia BCE, various local cultures that sprang up between the two major rivers started to slowly merge into one melting pot through trade, warfare, and other contacts. Their societies became more complex, with a ruling class on top, together with kings and shamans, and the working class on the bottom, mainly farmers. The first cities in the Chinese heartland were created, and around that time, China entered the Copper Age, abandoning stone for more advanced metal tools and weapons, which was a transition from the Neolithic to the Bronze Age. This was the beginning of what could be called proto-Chinese civilization.

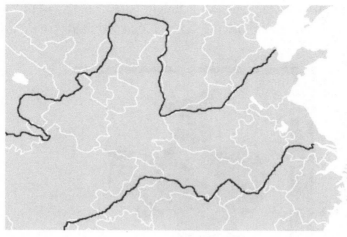

2. Map of central China with marked Yellow and Yangtze Rivers with modern provinces. Source: https://commons.wikimedia.org

Unfortunately for historians, the entire 3rd millennia BCE is shrouded by the numerous myths and legends that were written down in the later generations, and with only limited archeological findings, it is rather difficult to piece the exact events. Stories written down by early Chinese historians, like Sima Qian, tell us that in the early days the Three Sovereigns ruled one after another after the death of Pangu, and they were credited with creating order in the newly formed universe. They supposedly separated humans into tribes, gave them suitable rulers, organized the moving of the sun and the moon, and divided China into nine traditional provinces. These were some of the many feats attributed to them. These earliest rulers were seen as semi-divine, living for many thousands of years, having supernatural features, strength, and other inhuman characteristics. After them came the Five Emperors, starting with the Yellow Emperor. Traditionally his rule is dated to somewhere between 2700 and 2600 BCE, and he was often seen as the father of the Chinese people. He was the first who gave an order to the life of humans, teaching his nomadic brethren how to build shelters, farm, tame animals, and make clothes. He even gave them their first laws, the first version of the modern Chinese calendar, and taught them early math and writing. In essence, the myths tell us that he had created the Chinese civilization.

3. Ancient drawing depicting the Yellow Emperor.
Source: https://commons.wikimedia.org

But as he was a mere human, he died after reaching 113 years of life, leaving the throne to the next emperor. The next four emperors also ruled for a long time, most of them also managing to celebrate over 100 birthdays. And all of them were also very wise, capable rulers who further developed and bettered the life of the people. They brought music, art, and games (such as the traditional board game Weiqi, or Go), as well as regulated the social system into a patriarchal feudalism, forbade inter-kin marriage, and organized early religion. All of them also supposedly gave up their thrones willingly to the people they deemed more virtuous and worthier to rule. And interestingly the successors they chose were usually not from their families. The last emperor, Shun, gave his throne to Yu, today known as Yu the Great, who was a proven hero who managed to subdue the floods that troubled China at the time by building canals and dams, essentially creating the irrigation systems. As such, he was seen as a perfect man to continue the enlightened rule of the previous emperors aiming to further develop China. Traditionally his rule is dated somewhere between around 2200 and 2100 BCE, and he was seen as the ideal ruler, a wise philosopher king, who managed to unite various tribes, impose fair taxes, build roads, and distribute food, making China under his rule a land of overall welfare.

These stories of great mythical emperors are easily dismissible as pure fiction that was created in later centuries when they were written down, especially considering no concrete evidence of their rule has been found yet. No records remain, no tombs have been excavated, and not even a monument of some sort dating from their era has been uncovered. And for a long time, they have been dismissed by historians as nothing more than legends. But with new archeological findings, their interpretations have changed. Now they think these myths were actually based in reality in some aspects. During the 3rd millennia, Chinese civilization did go through its forming period, achieving almost all of the aforementioned feats of the great emperors. Their society started its stratification, where slowly a ruling class started to emerge; shamans and religion had been formed; they created their own calendar; and they showed early signs of writing, though they had not yet fully developed a writing system. Villages built irrigation systems allowing for better yields of crops which could withstand a larger population, leading to the growth of larger societies. Also, roads and early transportation devices like chariots and boats were built, which led to a tighter connection between different tribes and villages. The ceramics were now more delicate, with nicer decorations, while jade ware, now synonymous with Chinese classical art, have been found in tombs. This shows that the leap in the division of labor had been made at this time as this shows that there were artisans focused solely on their crafts.

Yet despite all those developments depicted in the stories, historians deduced that the society still hadn't moved on from the egalitarian clan system, where every member of the community was more or less equal to one another both in wealth and in position, precisely because in the stories mythical emperors weren't succeeded by their kids. They think that the ruling class still wasn't strong enough to enforce the hereditary rule, as most things, like land and cattle, were still shared among the tribe folk. But that separation did start during the 3rd millennia BCE, and according to the traditional Chinese chronology, it culminated around 2070 BCE when the last great emperor Yu left his throne to his son Qi. This leads historians to conclude that around that era a clear separation between the tribal elite, with a ruler at its head, and the commoners was achieved, leading China into the monarchical system. This moment also marks the birth of the first Chinese dynasty called Xia, starting the common division of Chinese history based on the ruling family. But even the historicity of the Xia has been questioned by many historians, as for a long time there was no direct evidence for their existence. Yet in the past several decades, new findings in the region where they supposedly ruled have shown that there was indeed a strong culture or a state that ruled over the lands mentioned in the myths, but no markings have been found clearly stating it was the Xia Dynasty.

4. Medieval painting of King Yu. Source: https://commons.wikimedia.org

Archeologists have found various vases, figurines, and other craftworks that indicate a rather sophisticated culture existed around the Yellow River at the beginning of the 2nd millennia BCE, along with new tools and weapons made out of bronze, clearly marking a point when China entered the Bronze Age. Also, some larger building projects, like royal palaces, have been unearthed in recent archeological surveys, with some historians suggesting that one of these sites may have been a Xia Dynasty capital. Now, these facts show us that roughly 4,000 years ago China lost the marks of the egalitarian tribal society completely. The ruling class became wealthy and powerful enough to command the commoners to build palaces, temples, or any other type of public works. Also, new technologies were adopted, most notably the casting of bronze, showing a rather important advance of the Chinese civilization. That combined with a more precise calendar allowed this supposed Xia culture to achieve a leap in farming production. And bronze weapons found clearly show that warfare became a more common thing among the ancient Chinese, which is also important for the social structure of the society, as the elites were tasked with the defense of the common population. But offensive wars also brought extra gains for the ruling class, further elevating them from the farmers and craftsmen.

Going back to the traditional sources, they tell us pretty much the same thing. Xia kings built palaces, waged wars with surrounding tribes, and expanded their territories, with a clear distinction developing between the rulers and elites from the commoners. These sources say that the Xia roughly ruled for 450 years. Their kings had their ups and downs, some being capable rulers, while others were either weak or abusive. But in the end, the entire dynasty has been held in high regard by the Chinese people throughout the centuries, with most of their rulers seen as the founding fathers of China. Their rule ended around 1600 BCE when one of the Xia vassals rebelled and overthrew Jie, the last Xia ruler, who was depicted as an abusive and poor ruler. That rebellious subject was Tang, the founder of the second Chinese dynasty called Shang. Today, the Xia Dynasty is still a controversial topic in Chinese history as some historians still see it as pure myth. A new theory has been proposed which states that the Xia did exist, but that they didn't actually rule over the entirety of China. Proponents of this theory point out that it is likely that later historians attributed that position to them, as in fact, the Xia state was the most powerful at the time, and its achievements were the best choice for historians to describe that period. In fact, they point out that according to the legends, the Shang and Zhou, the dynasties that came after the Xia, existed during the rule of that first dynasty.

In the end, choosing to believe in the stories of the Five Emperors or the Xia Dynasty isn't what is exactly important here. It is the fact that during the period described through these myths Chinese civilization was forged and formed into what we know today. These legends only tell us how the ancient Chinese themselves saw this transition through mythical and semi-mythical figures that led them from being wandering hunter-gatherers with stone tools to fully functional states and societies, armed with bronze and living in lavish palaces. And the ancient Chinese people have celebrated achievements of these long-gone ancestors, giving them due credit for all later accomplishments of Chinese culture. Finally, both these stories and the archeological evidence tell us one very important thing—how China was born.

Chapter 2 – Shang and Zhou Dynasties and the Rise of Royal Power

By the end of the 17ᵗʰ century BCE, the first Chinese dynasty had fallen and a new one had risen. The Shang Dynasty is the first historically confirmed dynasty that historians can clearly identify. It was also located in the basin of the Yellow River, continuing traditions and development of the Xia that came before them. And if the Xia did indeed build the foundations of Chinese civilization, the Shang were the ones that actually built it into what it is today. Under their reign, the imperial reign was solidified, further advances with bronze making and building were achieved, the calendar was further improved, and the writing system had been fully organized. And indeed, it is during the Shang Dynasty that China had gone from the prehistoric age to the age of recorded history, quickly rising from its humble beginnings into a civilization that could match any of its contemporaries.

That rise came with Tang, the first ruler of the Shang Dynasty, who at first was only a local subordinate of the Xia. Traditional histories tell us that he slowly gathered power and influence over the decades, mostly at the cost of the other Xia vassals. Slowly one by one, surrounding petty kingdoms, cities, and tribes fell under his rule, all while his suzerain, his feudal overlord, cared little. On the other hand, people and states that Tang conquered put up little resistance as Jie, the last Xia ruler, was a rather tyrannical king that cared little about his subordinates. Eventually, Tang's power grew and Jie's diminished, so the former vassal raised up against his superior and challenged his rule. When the battle was about to start, Tang gave a speech to his enemies, pointing out all of Jie's flaws, and according to tradition, many of the generals switched sides while common soldiers simply fled the battlefield. The Shang were victorious, and Jie had to run away, abandoning his throne. He spent the remaining years of his life in a monastery. And the new Shang Dynasty came to the throne. The exact year of this event is unknown; traditional history tells us it happened in the early 17th century, around 1675 BCE. But modern archeological surveys and in-depth analysis of the early Chinese histories indicate that it is more likely this happened somewhere around 1600.

The new Chinese ruler kept his word, and he first lowered taxes and reduced conscription for the royal army, making him more popular among the people. But despite the smaller army, Tang managed to widen his influence to surrounding tribes, actually increasing the size of the Shang state, ruling over the middle and lower Yellow River basin. And when the droughts burdened his people, he gave them money from his treasury to help them get by. For all of this, he is remembered as one of the best ancient Chinese kings. Yet regardless of this great start, it seems the early Shang Dynasty lacked stability as in the next 250 years their rulers changed the location of their capitals 5 times. Historians can't say why this happened, but it's most likely that the Shang rule wasn't secure and that they had to deal with many local and possibly external threats, so their rulers moved their capital across the country to either better deal with those problems or to establish their courts in more secure locations. But it seems that around 1350 BCE, Shang rulers managed to overcome these difficulties as King Pan Geng moved the Shang capital for the last time. He chose to return it to original capital of Tang, a location today called Anyang. This marked the start of the Shang golden age.

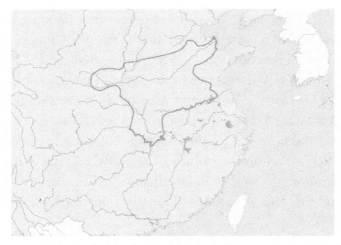

5. Map showing the territory of Shang Dynasty.
Source: https://commons.wikimedia.org

That golden age was marked by peace, prosperity, and an overall rise in the might of the Shang state, achieved while Pan Geng was still alive. Some of the later Chinese records even tell us that he brought back some of Tang's reforms, both to appease his subjects and to restore his kingdom to its previous glory. After Pan's death, he was succeeded by his two younger brothers before his nephew, Wu Ding, came to the throne, under whose rule the Shang achieved their greatest success. His reign has been more precisely dated by modern historians, and it lasted for an astonishing 58 years from 1250 to 1192 BCE. He was both a capable diplomat and a great military commander. He managed to establish and reinforce alliances with many surrounding tribes by marrying one of the princesses from each tribe, making all of them his concubines. And those tribes which were too hostile and warmongering Wu Ding pacified and conquered through war. He conquered three neighboring tribes, while another two after seeing his might chose to send emissaries and negotiate for peace, fearing they might be next. Of course, that kind of power also meant that economically the Shang state flourished, both from trade and from a rise in quantity and quality of production of all sorts.

Astonishing advances achieved by the golden era Shang Dynasty can be corroborated by archeological evidence as well. In royal tombs of this period, hundreds of finely made bronze items like wine cups, chalices, religious vessels, weapons, and even chariot decorations have been discovered. Beside those various items made out of bronze, ivory and other more luxurious materials were found. Such rich findings certainly show how wealthy the elite had become at the height of Shang power. But more important were the quantities of bronze found in these tombs, some measuring in tons, which show how developed Chinese metallurgy had become. No other ancient civilization has produced as much bronze as Shang China did. That leads historians to believe that from the small-scale bronze production of the Xia era, China managed to develop large-scale production by 15th century BCE, creating something that in modern terms we would call proto-industry. Agriculture was booming as well, with sources mentioning that Shang rulers were draining lowland swampy fields and clearing wild vegetation from fertile lands. This meant that food production was rising as well, explaining how the last Shang capital managed to boast a population of an estimated 140,000 people in its heyday.

6. Shang period bronze tripod. Source: https://commons.wikimedia.org

Another sign of prosperity of the Shang state, or at least of its ruling elite, was the number of animal offerings in the temples.

Usually, about ten head of cattle would be sacrificed, but for special occasions, these numbers would rise into the hundreds. And cattle weren't the only animals sacrificed. Ancient Chinese offered sheep, pigs, and even dogs to their gods. Of course, most of these animals and the pastures they fed upon were in the hands of the royal family and the elite, and it is highly unlikely that the commoners enjoyed as much meat as their rulers did.

But despite how important the development of large-scale animal husbandry was to the Chinese civilization, it could be argued that the introduction of horses and chariots was more important. Current evidence suggests that this important advancement happened in the 13th century, most likely through the nomadic tribes that lived in the Central Asian steppes, as the domestication of horses first occurred in the Caucasus and the Middle East. Domestication and use of horses were important advances that made travel easier and faster, and they were also useful as work animals and for the transport of goods. As for the chariots, at first they were used only for hunting and as mobile command vehicles in battles, but as the Shang Dynasty was approaching its end, the use of chariots in battles became more widespread and more directly used, participating in a fight instead of just staying in the back merely as a command post.

It was also during the rule of the Shang that war and military became more important and better organized even though the size of their armies, usually ranging from three to five thousand and rarely going up to ten thousand, wasn't that impressive. Most of the warriors were foot soldiers armed with axes, spears, and bows. At the core of these armies stood a small number of trained noble professionals, which can be attested by the existence of various titles and ranks, who spent their lives honing their fighting skills. And they most likely protected the king or the general in charge. The majority of the troops came from untrained peasant levies raised from the subordinate noble lineages called zu. These linages served as both military and social organizations, which give us glimpses into how the Shang state and society was organized. It was, in fact, a semi-feudal patriarchal lineage system in which royal lineage ruled over the smaller local families that were to serve their king. Lineage heads of these zu were interconnected with the royal dynasty through various kinship ties, benefits, privileges, and obligations. Kings offered them spiritual guidance, performing religious rituals for them, and protection for their service in his armies and for the tributes they paid. It becomes obvious that the Shang state still didn't have fully developed bureaucracy, as it depended on the local aristocracy to fulfill the will of the central government even though there were some royal offices, usually given to the higher nobles trusted by the king, like "junior servitor for cultivation." The question remains if these proto-bureaucratic offices actually held any power or were only ceremonial.

Another thing that this patriarchal social system also tells us is that the ancient Chinese kings served an important religious role in society. Calling upon their connection with their deified and worshiped ancestors, the Shang rulers managed to play a central role in the religious life of their subjects, which was an important cornerstone of their control over the subjects they ruled. This made early Chinese kings' rule rather theocratic, as it was with many other ancient kings, for example, the pharaohs in Egypt. This role of the king as a royal shaman, of course, decreased as their political power and wealth rose, as they no longer needed to rely as much upon spiritual control of the people beneath them. But despite that, religion continued to play an important role in the everyday life of Shang China. Sacrifices were a common practice for them, and though most of the offerings were animals or valuable items, in some cases there are signs of human sacrifices, mostly in royal tombs, possibly to serve the kings in the afterlife. And even in death, they preserved the hierarchy, with the closest retainers of the ruler being buried closest to him. Farthest away were dismembered and decapitated young men, most likely prisoners of war.

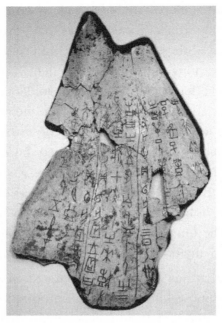

7. Oracle bones carved with earliest found evidence of the Chinese script.
Source: https://commons.wikimedia.org

Divination seemed to be one of the most important segments of their belief system and practices, where the shamans would try to speak with the gods and the ancestors, asking for their advice and favors. The importance of this practice is corroborated by the fact that the earliest evidence of the Chinese script comes from 13th century BCE oracle bones, where they would inscribe records and question which would then be burned and interpreted by a soothsayer through pyromantic divinations. Using written words for divination, at the time when literacy was uncommon and script was seen as something special and almost magical, means that this practice had a special significance for the ancient Chinese. And as bones are long-lasting materials, those writings were preserved from being lost in memory.

The fact that there was a fully developed writing system during the Shang rule is also indicative of how far the Chinese civilization had advanced by that point. Now it should be mentioned that it is most likely that the ancient Chinese had developed writing well before the 13th century, as by that time it was already a fully functional and organized system, with some historians arguing that the first versions of the Chinese script had been developed during the Xia Dynasty. But as no archeological evidence for that has been found, at this point it's only conjecture. Also, it should be noted that writing most likely wasn't used only for religious purposes, at least by the golden age of the Shang Dynasty. As their state was at that point rather large, with various tributes being paid and levies being raised, they needed to keep some records of all state business. Some evidence found in the script itself points to the possibility of non-religious documents being written on less durable materials like bamboo, wood, or even cloth, making their survival to the present day rather unlikely. But the fact remains that Chinese culture had advanced significantly by the late 2nd millennium BCE, attested not only by writing but with all the other achievements of the Shang Dynasty.

But as it is often the case in history, after a great ruler and a golden age, states usually start declining and the central government slowly loses its power. As time progressed, new kings of the Shang Dynasty were less and less involved with the ruling, delegating more and more to their officers. They were no longer generals leading their troops, and they no longer worried about the general wellbeing of their subjects, leaving their representatives to deal with droughts or famine. And as their grip loosened, with their focus on indulgence instead of ruling, vassals and subjects started to slowly slip away from their control. First farther away from the Shang core territory, then closer to home. One of these rogue vassals was the noble Zhou family, which ruled in the western borders of the Shang state. They became so powerful, almost to the point of being an independent state, that eventually the head of the family named Wen was imprisoned by a Shang king called Di Xin. He feared Wen's influence and might. As retribution, Wen planned to overthrow the Shang king, who in his youth was a rather good and capable ruler, but who became more and more careless and cruel in his older age. Yet Wen died before following through with his plans. But his son Wu fulfilled his father wishes.

As a king, Di Xin was unaware of just how bad the state of his dominion was, so he sent an army to battle in the east. Wu exploited this and attacked the core of the Shang territory, and according to traditional sources, he was backed by many former allies and loyal vassals of the decaying Shang Dynasty. In 1046 BCE, the grand battle of Muye ensued in which forces of Di Xin suffered a complete defeat. He fled to one of his palaces where he set himself on fire, committing suicide. With his death, Wu became the new king, creating a new dynasty called Zhou. And the old Shang king, who became one of the examples of a bad and corrupt ruler, actually became known as King Zhou, which when written in different Chinese characters and pronounced differently means horse crupper, a part of the saddle which was most often soiled by the horse. At this point, it seemed that the rule of the new Zhou Dynasty was secured, as most of the people welcomed the change on the throne, especially as the new king immediately opened royal warehouses to help the troubled commoners and gain their support. But only two years after his great victory, King Wu died, leaving only his rather young son named Song to rule.

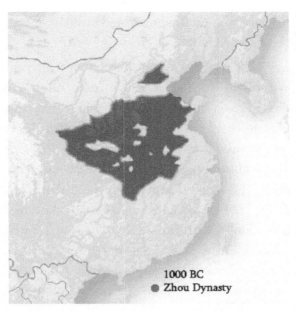

1000 BC
● Zhou Dynasty

8. Territory under Zhou rule around 1000 BCE
Source: https://commons.wikimedia.org

Fearing that a young king may be a liability on the throne as the Zhou Dynasty rule was not yet cemented, his uncle Gong Dan stepped in as his guardian and regent, ruling in his place. But it seems this was Gong Dan's sole decision as other brothers of the late king Wu were angered by his move, as at least one of them had seniority in the succession line. This led to a civil war between brothers. On one side was Gong Dan and King Cheng, as Song became later known, and the "Three Guards," Gong Dan's brothers. And although the Guards were also backed by other nobles and the remnants of the Shang Dynasty, in the end, they were unable to beat Gong Dan. He used his power not only to confirm the rule of the Zhou Dynasty but also to expand its territory. And when young King Cheng became old enough, he willingly stepped down, leaving the throne to his nephew, but still remained an important part of the royal council. As such, he was remembered in the next generations as the paragon of virtue, sometimes even called The First Sage. But more importantly, some modern historians credit him for formulating the political doctrine known as the Mandate of Heaven.

That doctrine was used to legitimize the overthrowing of the Shang Dynasty and the formation of the new Zhou Dynasty. It stipulated that every dynasty and its current ruler had been given a mandate by heaven to rule in the natural order, for the benefit of the entire nation. If any ruler failed to do so, he could be rightfully dethroned and substituted by another, even substituting an entire dynasty with him. And as the last ruler of the Shang situation was rather terrible, the Zhou had all the right to rebel, as now the mandate from heaven was on their side, which was confirmed by their victory. This doctrine had since those days become one of the most important pillars of the imperial rule, which was upheld by all following dynasties going up to the 20th century and the modern age. It has been used by Chinese kings and emperors to both stabilize and consolidate their rule, as well as a justification to overthrow their predecessors. It is worth mentioning that though this was the first official proclamation of this doctrine, its roots can be traced to the stories of how the Shang overthrew the Xia Dynasty for their maleficent rule.

But the Zhou Dynasty did more than just rely on a new political doctrine to secure its newly acquired power. First, kings recognized that one of the weaknesses of the Shang state was disloyalty of the vassals, which had little real ties to the central government. The Zhou rulers realized that relying on religion and offering protection wasn't going to buy them much loyalty, so they confiscated and divided a lot of lands among their next of kin, to the brothers and sons of kings Wu and Cheng, as well as Gong Dan. This created dozens of smaller city-states, which were closely connected to the central dynasty by blood. This kind of decentralized rule, where local lords govern their own estates with only partial subordination to the central government, is sometimes equated to the medieval European feudalism, but that is not the case here. This system, known as fēngjiàn, was more based on familial ties than on the feudal code. And at best it could be described as proto-feudalism. And indeed, it brought a few decades of peace and prosperity in China, without many rivalries and fights among the nobles, as they did not challenge the authority of the central government.

9. King Zhao of Zhou. Source: https://commons.wikimedia.org

This early period is marked by the expansion and conquest of the neighboring tribes to the north and the east. And these newly conquered lands weren't just forced into vassalage, as was the custom before. The new dynasty tried to maintain a higher level of control and loyalty from these areas by colonizing them, giving the local rule to their family members and relocating some of the loyal population with them. It was a sign that the new fēngjiàn system was functioning, as the Zhou state became more powerful, wealthier, and larger than their Shang predecessor. But in the mid-10th century BCE, under the rule of King Zhao, who ruled from 977 to 957, expansion was halted. He tried to continue in the footsteps of his father and grandfather, but he suffered a decisive defeat in his campaign in the south. The Zhou Dynasty lost both its ruler and the majority of the core royal forces. Zhao's successor king, Mu, found himself in a tough position. The central government lost both its might and its reputation among their subjects. At the same time, due to the changing of generations, the blood connection between the king and his vassals thinned down, as the ties were no longer as close as brothers and uncles; now they became distant cousins twice or thrice removed. The Zhou proto-feudal system was starting to crack.

And it seems that King Mu was aware of that as he worked hard to reform the state, starting with the army. He realized that it would be more beneficial if he chose his captains and generals according to their abilities rather than due to their familial ties. Thus, he started the practice of investiture in the army, which marked a start of Chinese military restructuring and a gradual turn toward professionalization. Mu used a similar idea when he reformed his court as well. He gathered capable people around him to act as his ministers or, as they were titled, supervisors, alongside numerous scribes, attendants, and provisioners. Thus, a bureaucratic apparatus was created that started to separate the king from his people, even the nobles. This could be clearly seen in the fact that during his reign all visitors of the royal court had to be introduced to the king who no longer knew all of his vassals personally. Furthermore, King Mu started the practice of writing down every court decision, ruling, maps, investitures, laws, and any other royal action. By doing that, he created the first systematical legal code in China.

These reforms allowed King Mu to spend most of his long rule in campaigns with his army. He waged wars on pretty much all fronts. He defended then expanded the western and northern borders, confirmed the royal influence in the east, and led a successful invasion in the southeast. He was rather successful in those military actions, as under his rule the Zhou state achieved its greatest extent. He managed to conquer numerous tribes either by swaying their allegiance with the showing of the royal force or through pure conquest if they refused to comply. But despite his military success and important reforms, he wasn't seen as a great ruler. On the one hand, he received due praise for his achievements but on the other, he was criticized for being away from the capital too often, and that his legal and bureaucratic reforms were needed because he lacked the virtues and charisma of previous rulers. And during his reign, the rule of the kings became a faceless, distant administrative system which cared less for the people. Even his military achievements were seen only as a partial success as one of the larger border states stopped being a royal vassal.

Yet despite the flaws of King Mu, he did manage to keep his rule mostly stable, and the central government retained both influence and power. But during the next half-century and the next four Chinese kings, those things slowly but surely changed. Though exact chronology and events can't be precisely dated, certain stories give us glimpses into how the general state of affairs developed. One of the most important eastern vassals was boiled in oil, and on several occasions, the royal army had to interfere in local affairs of the nobles. This means that the control of the central government was deteriorating and that now it had to rely on brute force to enforce its own will. Some of the vassals even dared attack the royal lands. At the same time, surrounding tribes were also using the weakened state of China as a reason to attack it. Later sources tell us that the royal house started to decline, even being ridiculed by satires of poets. The culmination of that deterioration came during the rule of King Li in the mid-9th century BCE.

King Li was a terrible king, corrupt and decadent, without a single redeeming quality. He cared little about his subjects, refused to listen to the advice of his court officials or other nobles, seeking only ways to gather more wealth. King Li was also cruel, severely punishing anyone who dared to speak out against him. Things became so unbearable that finally some of the nobles started an open revolt against the Zhou, forcing King Li into exile in 841 BCE. The period that ensued is today known as the Gonghe (joint harmony) Regency where the Chinese throne was factually empty. During this interregnum, it seems that a certain Gong He ruled as a regent, though some sources also mentioned a combined rule of Shao Gong and Zhou Gong. But even if the latter two weren't ruling, they played an important role at the time as in 828, when King Li died in exile, they persuaded Gong He to give up the rule in favor of Li's son, the future king Xuan. The Gonghe Regency gives us a sure clue how weakened the royal power had become by that time and how powerful the nobles became. But despite that, some of the royal prestige and significance remained, otherwise Xuan wouldn't have been chosen to rule, as Gong He was in a good position to start a new dynasty. Most likely he wasn't able to do so as other nobles would have opposed him.

Whatever may be the actual reason, King Xuan assumed the throne, and at first, he seemed like the capable and strong leader the Zhou needed to recover from the interregnum. In the first third of his 45-year rule, he achieved substantial victories in the west and the south, while he managed to reaffirm the Zhou control in the east. His main goal was to restore the royal authority, and it seemed he was going to achieve it. But as the years passed, the Zhou king once again got the military involved in succession matters of the local lords on several occasions. It is likely that he was trying to ensure that his supporters and people more loyal to him would inherit the titles, thus widening the support he had among the nobles. But this plan backfired, and after these interventions, most of the nobles started rebelling, refusing to carry out orders that came from the king and the central government. This eventually led to his downfall, as he stepped out of line by killing an innocent nobleman. Legends say

King Xuan was eventually killed by the angry ghost of the murdered noble, but in reality, it was most likely assassination in retribution for the vile act. So, in 782 BCE he was succeeded by his son, You.

10. *King Xuan of Zhou. Source: https://commons.wikimedia.org*

The reign of the new king started rather ominously as a major earthquake caused massive damage in the second year of his rule. Sources tell us that mountains crumbled and rivers dried out, and even though this is most likely an exaggeration, it shows that there were severe consequences of this natural disaster. To make matters worse, he caused troubles in his court as he chased off his queen and heir, who came from an important noble family, in favor of a concubine and a son he had with her. Traditional histories tell us that furthermore King You toyed with the remaining loyal nobles by lighting alarm beacons for the amusement of his concubine queen. And soon no one answered the call of the alarm. So, when in 771 BCE the former queen's family colluded with the western barbarian tribes, which were a constant threat for the Zhou capital for decades, and attacked, no one came to help the foolish king. He was murdered, and the capital was ransacked and devastated. With the death of King You, the main branch of the Zhou Dynasty was now extinguished, and Ping, the son of the banished queen, became the new king. Since the region was brutally sacked by the barbarians, the capital was moved to the east, where one of the early Zhou colonies were created. This marks a fall of the so-called Western Zhou and the start of the Eastern Zhou Dynasty.

Even though in reality the same dynasty remained in power, many modern historians see this moment as pivotal in the further development of Chinese history. With a new king, a new capital, and rather important changes in royal power, historians tend to divide the Zhou rule into two separate periods. As it will become clear in the next chapter, during the Eastern Zhou rule, royal power and dynastic prestige would continue to fade, leaving only an empty shell of its former glory. But despite that ungraceful development, the early Western Zhou rulers did leave an important mark on China and its political development. Under their almost three centuries-long rule, the dogma of the government property and control, political thoughts and doctrines, and even of poetic expressions were established. All of this became embedded into the Chinese culture and intellectual thought, present even today in some form. And if the Xia and Shang Dynasties were the foundations of the Chinese civilization, often unseen and buried under the soil of forgotten history, the Western Zhou are a visible and recognizable cornerstone, marking the base of future Chinese grandeur. And for that they deserved, and indeed received, eternal praise of the Chinese people.

Chapter 3 – Disintegration of Royal Power

Despite the fact that the Eastern Zhou survived, carrying on the traditions set by the early Zhou kings, by the late 8th century BCE, it became clear that the royal power of the ruling dynasty had all but disappeared. In fact, for the most part of the next five centuries, Zhou rulers were mostly only puppets on the throne, while the real power lay with local nobles ruling the several large states. This is why historians sometimes disregard the Eastern Zhou Dynasty, dividing their formal rule into two periods. First was the Autumn and Spring Period, named after the Spring and Autumn Annals, which describe the period between 722 and 481 in which nobles competed for the influence over the king. The other period is known as the Warring States Period, which lasted until 221, in which the nobles openly fought amongst themselves for full control of China, without much regard for the actual Zhou ruler. But the disintegration of the royal power started in 771 when the capital was moved to the east and when the core Zhou lands were abandoned by the king.

King Ping, who was responsible for the relocation of the royal capital, in the early days of his reign, forged an alliance with one of the more important noble families called Zheng. In fact, the Zheng forces protected the court while it was moving to the east, and later they defended royal lands from the barbarian invasion. But at the same time, the Zheng duke disregarded any formal relations between him and his liege, attacking other Zhou vassals. Ping tried to balance Zheng power by appointing another mighty noble, the Duke of Guo, to an important court minister office. The Duke of Zheng was enraged, and in an attempt to pacify him, the Zhou king proposed an exchange of hostages between him and the duke. This was an unheard-of precedent in the fēngjiàn feudal system, showing once more how the royal power had wavered.

In 719, Ping died, and his son Huan became the new king. Like his father, he feared the might of the Zheng duke, so he tried once again to limit his influence by placing a Guo noble as his chief minister. This time the Duke of Zheng responded by openly attacking the king's lands. In response, King Huan gathered forces of several other vassals and in 707 fought against the rebellious duke. The Zhou forces were defeated, and this marked the end of any kind of royal authority, especially as the king himself was wounded. That fact meant that the Zhou kings lost their status as the Sons of Heaven.

It was in this political atmosphere that the rule of Eastern Zhou started, with about 150 independent states only formally subordinated to the kings. Of course, most of these states were rather small, consisting of only one city and its immediate surroundings. Most of these smaller states were annexed by one of the fifteen larger states. And out of those fifteen, only the Chu, Jin, Qi, and Qin states were constantly competing for the leading role among the states, for power, influence, and prestige during the Autumn and Spring Period. Of course, the other states were also involved as allies and foes, or simply as battlegrounds between the major powers. And as before, they were all surrounded by the barbarian tribes which were a constant threat to the Chinese states, but also possible allies in the struggle for power. The Duke of Zheng tried to enforce himself as the de facto leader of China after his victory over the Zhou forces, but he died before he could fully achieve that. And as he had many sons, his successors started fighting amongst themselves as who would become the next Duke of Zheng. Rather quickly, other states got involved in these skirmishes as well. That civil war, combined with lack of any signs of Zhou power, prompted several barbarian tribes to invade the Yellow River Valley.

11. Map of states and territories of the Eastern Zhou period.
Source: https://commons.wikimedia.org

But where the Duke of Zheng failed, the Duke Huan of Qi succeeded. In 685 BCE, he became the duke of the eastern state of Qi, and with the help of his chief minister, he reformed his domain. With a more hierarchical administration, which was now better organized and more efficient, Qi became capable of mobilizing human and material resources better than any other state, making it the most powerful in the entire Chinese realm. By 667, Duke Huan was powerful enough to gather rulers of four other states which all pledged allegiance to him. At the same time, the Zhou King Hui had been challenged by his brother for the throne. Seeing how Duke Huan was the most powerful leader, he asked for his assistance in exchange for a title he created just for him, the title of ba (hegemon). Huan accepted, as that title legally recognized his leadership among the Chinese states, and it gave him the right to intervene militarily in the name of the royal court as he pleased. Though this would seem like a usurpation of the royal power, it seems Duke Huan and his chief minister didn't plan for that. The goal of their hegemony was to preserve the

Zhou feudal system and restore the authority of the Son of Heaven.

The actions of Duke of Qi, in essence, corroborate these intentions as he attacked a state that supported the king's brother, sent armies to help smaller states against the barbarian invaders, and even helped reestablish several states that had been practically destroyed by the foreign invaders. These actions cemented his place as the head of the Chinese states. But at the same time, the southern state of Chu, which remained outside of the Zhou feudal system, grew stronger and started to expand to the north. It became a serious threat to all the other states, so in 656, Duke Huan led an allied army of eight northern states against them, beating them in open battle. With that victory, he forced Chu to negotiate, stopping their expansion for the time being. But the biggest success of the Duke of Qi was a series of interstate meetings, the most important being the one held in 651 in Kuiqui. There several major states agreed to respect the patriarchal traditions of old, attempting to stop the political chaos when it came to the question of succession. They also agreed upon respecting each other's boundaries, preserving irrigation systems, and promoting the trade of grain, which was aimed at improving state relations. But at the same time, an agreement made at Kuiqui stipulated that no administrative office should be hereditary, promoting the meritocratic system against the old feudal ideals.

Unfortunately for Qi, Duke Huan died in 643, leaving behind six sons who immediately started fighting for succession despite their father's attempts to prevent exactly that. For that, the state of Qi lost its place as the hegemon. It was unofficially succeeded by the state of Song, led by Duke Xiang. For a short period, the state of Song was the most powerful, even intervening in matters of succession in Qi. But in 638, Xiang attempted, against the advice of his officers, to lead his army against the state of Chu. He was defeated, dying a year later from the wounds sustained in battle, and Song's power was destroyed. But despite the fact Xiang never officially received the title of ba from the Zhou king, his attempts to continue in the footsteps of Duke Huan led the ensuing generations of Chinese to count him as one of the Zhou hegemons. During the same period, the northern state of Jin also went through reforms under the rule of Duke Wen, and it rapidly became one of the most powerful Chinese states. So, in 635 when King Xiang needed an ally to keep his throne in a struggle with his brother, Wen was glad to help. Then he led the allied army against the invading forces of Chu in 633 and achieved an important victory. That helped earn him the title of hegemon in 632.

In his attempts to retain a balance of power, the leader of Jin fought off the expansion of the Qin state to the east. But Duke Wen died shortly after in 628, and Duke Mu of Qin exploited that and continued his expansion, achieving a major victory over the state of Jin in 624. Like the previous hegemon states, Qin also went through reforms before achieving its supremacy, no matter how short it lasted. Its core lands were in the valley of the Wei River, where the Western Zhou Dynasty was situated before. As such, it managed to expand both to the barbarian tribes to the west as well as to the smaller states that lay to the east of it. Once again, Duke Mu was never officially recognized as a hegemon, but his superiority until his death in 621 made later generations recognize him as one. From that point onward, it seems that no state managed to gain the upper hand as all skirmishes between Qi, Qin, and Jin ended without a decisive victory. And soon after the southern state of Chu was once again advancing to the north, under the rule of self-proclaimed king Zhuang. In 598, he managed to defeat the forces of Jin and even endangered the realm of the Zhou king. But despite the fact that the leader of Chu was the most powerful of all the rulers, he also didn't receive official recognition but is still counted as one of the hegemons, like several rulers before him.

He died in 591, and the struggle for power continued with all of the four most powerful states being approximately equal in power and influence, especially when the state of Jin connected with the state of Wu in the lower reaches of the Yangzi River. This state before this point was seen as barbaric and wasn't part of Chinese civilizational reach. But Jin saw potential in it, helping it with arms and technology so it could threaten the state of Chu on a new front. But this wasn't enough to stop the ever-growing power of Chu, so in 580 BCE, the state of Jin managed to once again forge an alliance with Qi and Qin to fight against the southern threat. With that, the four major states were in a deadlock, and the state of Song that was caught between them convinced them to arrange a meeting the following year. There they agreed on peace and disarmament, limiting their military powers, which is one of the earliest records of this kind of agreement. Yet it was short-lived as by 575 the full-scale war continued with a victory for Jin and its allies against Chu. Under the rule of a new duke named Dao, the state of Jin went through a new set of reforms, further developing a meritocratic administrative system. That gave this state internal stability, and its achievements against the Chu and some barbarian tribes was enough for Dao to become the next ba.

But by that time, the Zhou kings lost any kind of respect to other dukes and rulers, so his title of hegemon meant almost nothing anymore. And the fighting continued over the next several decades. This kind of never-ending warfare became rather exhausting, especially for the smaller states that served as little more than the battlefields for the major powers, and this led to another meeting of the four major powers in 546. However, this time they were accompanied by several smaller states as well. There, in essence, the spheres of influence of these states were agreed upon, and peace among them ensued for several decades with only smaller skirmishes among their vassals. But by no means did this mean ultimate peace was achieved. Despite peace on its northern borders, Chu had to fight in the south against former allies of Jin, the state of Wu. For a long time, Wu harassed the bordering provinces of Chu, slowly exhausting its enemy. By 506, the state of Wu felt powerful enough to launch a full-scale attack on Chu, bringing it on the verge of collapse in the next couple of years. But before the final blow was struck, the Wu capital was attacked by Yue forces, another new power in the southern edges of the Chinese world.

This forced the ruler of Wu, who like the rulers of Chu held the title of king which wasn't recognized by the dukes of the northern states, to rush back and defend his land. He succeeded but died from the wounds sustained from the fight. His son, King Fuchai, avenged his father in 494. He forced the king of Yue to surrender to him. With secure southern borders, the army of Wu marched to the north. There they fought against the forces of Qi and won, while at the same time Fuchai attempted to build a canal to connect the Central Plain, which is another name for the region between the Yellow and Yangtze Rivers, with the southern states. This was a direct challenge to Jin, the most powerful northern state, which yielded, deciding not to confront the mighty army of Wu. This prompted King Fuchai to preside over an interstate conference in 482 where he was awarded the title of ba. But while his armies were busy in the north, the king of Yue launched a new attack on the capital of Wu, prompting the king of Wu to rush back south once more. His new title meant nothing when his forces were defeated by King Goujian of Yue. The Yue forces did retreat after a peace treaty, but King Goujian didn't want to let Wu recuperate from the defeat, so soon after he launched a new invasion. By 473, Wu was completely defeated, and Fuchai committed suicide. Afterward, Goujian marched north and was recognized as the new hegemon. But this title lost almost all of its weight, and with his death in 465 BCE, the ba system came to an end.

12. Spear of King Fuchai of Wu. Source: https://commons.wikimedia.org

With the disintegration of the ba system, the disappearance of over 120 smaller states, and the total annihilation of royal authority, the Spring and Autumn Period ended. The exact end year is debated among historians, ranging from 481 to 403 BCE, but most commonly the year used is the one proposed by the ancient Chinese historian, Sima Qian, who said it happened in 476. But the year isn't what is really important, but how Chinese civilization changed in those three centuries. Maybe most importantly, the old familial feudal system was largely abolished and substituted by a meritocratic system, even for higher court official positions and the most important fiefs, as the most capable people became ministers that in some cases played an important role in the development of the states they served. And later on, as there was less and less land to give, it became harder for new aristocratic families to rise, making it a rather closed circle.

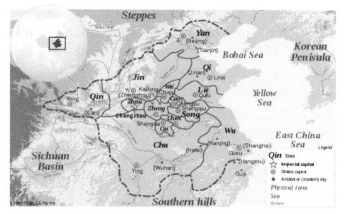

13. *States of the late Spring and Autumn Period.*
Source: https://commons.wikimedia.org

Another step away from the feudal system was the development of an advanced administrative system, where the meritocratic system was most useful. State territories were divided into a number of smaller administrative regions ruled by governors who directly answered to the ruler, and whose office wasn't hereditary. They were helped by local administrative personnel, like sheriffs and stewards. This was important because it made levying the troops easier as well as broader, giving dukes and kings of the late Spring and Autumn Period much larger armies at their disposal. This stems from the fact that in earlier times they could levy troops only from their capital, but now the entire land was at their disposal. But probably more important than that was the fact that this kind of advanced administrative system allowed for better taxation, allowing for more money to flow into the rulers' treasuries. This was accompanied by reforming the taxes so that the sum the state required depended on the size of arable land. Amount of levied taxes also rose with the increase of farming output that happened during this period. One of the reasons for this was, once again, because the old feudal system was failing. In the old Zhou system, in theory, all land belonged to the king, and peasants had little incentive to work harder than they had to. But as the royal authority disappeared, slowly farmers gained the right of tenure and later even ownership, making them more productive. This was coupled with the advances in farming techniques and technologies that also happened in this period. Among those was harnessing animals, mainly oxen, to pull the plows, allowing for deeper cuts into the soil. Coupled with that was the use of metal iron tools, which also made farming more efficient.

That fact also tells us that during this period China was transitioning from the Bronze Age to the Iron Age, though this transformation was not yet complete. At the time, iron was still of a lesser quality, and it was mostly used for tools, while bronze was considered "fine metal." As such, it was still used for weapons and ceremonial items. But both types of metal were made with the casting technology, which made mass production easier. They were melted and produced in kilns that could reach up to $1300\,°C$ ($2370°F$). Not coincidentally, during this same period, pottery techniques advanced enough for its products to be called ceramics. And in most cities from this period, archeologist have found remains of bronze-making and pottery workshops, meaning that these industries, if it's possible to call them that, were an important part of economic life in ancient China. With more food surpluses and new "industrial" products came the rise of commerce, which also became an important part of the late Spring and Autumn Period. Development of trade also pushed for further improvements of the road networks which were secured and maintained by the state. The active exchange of material wealth through commerce also gave rise to an important advance in the Chinese civilization, the appearance of money, or to be more precise, minted coins. This helped to further improve trade and circulation of wealth, making economic life in ancient China livelier, pushing states into new heights.

14. Bronze polearm head of the Spring and Autumn Period.
Source: https://commons.wikimedia.org

All of these changes were accompanied by the change of Chinese philosophical and political thought. With state administration growing ever more complex and needing qualified people to run it, members of the elite slowly started to shift from a purely warrior class to a more intellectual one. And from that pool of talent, the best were chosen, thanks to the meritocratic system, to serve as high-ranking officers. Thanks to this, they were able to spearhead the intellectual development of ancient China. The best example of this is, of course, the world-famous Confucius, who served the state of Lu and managed to create a universal code of conduct applicable to everyone based on his interpretation of traditions and old feudal customs. His thoughts became one of the pillars of Chinese civilization, which still remains today. But despite the traditionalism he proclaimed, his thoughts were innovative and represented a more pragmatic approach in the Chinese political and intellectual thought. This can be corroborated by the fact that the old traditions, like relying on shamans to overcome droughts or on legends and customs to keep society in line, were weakening and losing their place in Chinese civilization. Instead, Confucianism rather relied on written codes of law. In general, it could be said that pragmatism started to permeate the Chinese society in the Spring and Autumn Period. But this civilization was only halfway through the processes of all of these changes, which were going to culminate in the next era, today known as the Warring States Period.

Chapter 4 – Birth of Imperial China

Though the Spring and Autumn Period seemed like a never-ending conflict between the Chinese states, it was actually a gradual preparation for a major escalation of warfare which culminated in the next epoch in Chinese history. It became known as the Warring States Period because the essence of war changed during it with battles becoming bloodier and campaigns lasting longer. Under that kind of pressure, the nature of the states changed as well, as they became territorial and bureaucratic in nature. Their number was further reduced as smaller states continued to be sucked in by the more powerful states. And while in the previous period there were only four major powers among the Chinese states, during the Warring States era their number rose to seven. These were Qin, Qi, Chu, Yan, Han, Zhao, and Wei. This period was characterized by large-scale warfare and alliances among these major states, three of which were old powers from the previous period.

At the beginning of this period, probably the most influential of the major states was the state of Qi, on the shores of present-day Bohai Sea, covering the area of modern Chinese provinces of Shandong and Hebei. Then there was the state of Chu in the south, covering an area around the Huai and Yangtze Rivers. In the west was Qin, located in the basin of the Wei River, which later expanded to the parts of the modern-day Sichuan province. Then there was a new major power in the north, around present-day Beijing, called the state of Yan, and it was the last state to emerge as a powerhouse. The final three were formed during the second half of the 5th century in a long process today known as the partition of Jin. This state, which throughout the Spring and Autumn Period was usually the most powerful, got mixed up in a long civil war that lasted from about 458 to 403, when three leading aristocratic families were recognized by the Zhou king, as well as other states, as equals. The smallest of these emerging states was Han, which covered the southern parts of modern-day Shanxi and Henan provinces. The second successor of Jin was the state of Zhao, located on the northern borders of China, on the borders of present-day Inner Mongolia and the northern parts of Shanxi provinces. And finally, the most powerful heir of Jin was Wei, a state located north of the Yellow River and in the valley of the Fen River, covering an area of the modern-day central Shanxi province, as well as parts of the Henan and Hebei provinces.

The early decades of the Warring States Period were marked by further reforms that started in the previous century that finally transformed Chinese states one by one into ruler-centered states. This meant that dukes became the sole source of authority in their states. The last states to achieve this kind of centralization of power were Qin, who gained it only at the beginning of the 4th century, and Yan, where these reforms were conducted at the end of that century. An exception was the state of Chu which never became fully ruler-centered, as they had a mixed strength with royal authority. This weakness was compensated by the sheer size of this southern state, which throughout this period remained the largest. Of course, this period was also marked by wars and skirmishes between the major states and their expansions, both through conquering remaining smaller states and through expanding into the "barbarian wilderness." The first state to benefit from the reforms was Qi, who in the mid-4th century managed to affirm itself as the strongest state after significant victories over Wei and Yen. But the most important result of these victories was the fact that in 344 rulers of Qi and Wei mutually recognized each other as kings, finally showing that the Zhou Dynasty lost the last remnants of its importance. From this point on, all states were interlocked in a fight to become the new supreme ruler of all Chinese states.

The Situation of Early Warring States Period

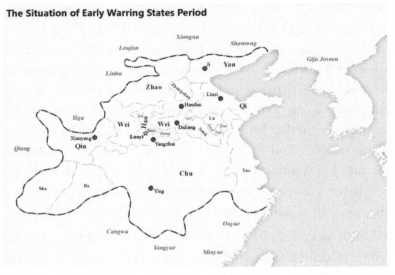

15. Map of China in the early Warring States Period.
Source: https://commons.wikimedia.org

But the higher ranked ruler state of Wei was actually going through a period of crisis, as the reformed and more powerful Qin started attacking it from the west. It suffered several defeats in the mid-4th century and had to rely on Qi to stop Qin from completely conquering it in 340. With this, the two most powerful states in ancient China became Qin and Qi. As a result, in 325, the ruler of Qin proclaimed himself king as well, and soon he was followed by rulers of Han, Zhao, and Yan in the next two years. And as rulers of Chu bore the unrecognized title of kings since the 7th century, this meant that all of the major states were now officially kingdoms, and they recognized each other in that way. What little dignity left for the Zhou kings was destroyed in the following years when rulers of smaller states, like Song and Zhongshan, also proclaimed themselves kings. Interestingly, after a considerable defeat of Zhao in a war with Qin in 318, the king of that state retracted his proclamation, returning his title to a level of a duke. Despite that, his son and successor held a tile of a king. Meanwhile, in the south, the state of Chu was conquering its only contender in the Yangtze River Valley, the state of You, strengthening its position.

By the late 4th and early 3rd century, the state of Qin grew to become the number one power in China that no other state, not even Chu or Qi, could match in a direct fight. This rise in might didn't just come from the state and military reforms, but mostly as a result of expansion in present-day Sichuan. This land in the upper region of the Yangtze River was rather fertile, giving a boost to the Qin economy and providing a fresh source of new troops. As a bonus, their lands were rather secure by mountain ranges, especially the new territories, so their lands suffered almost no damage from foreign invasions. And finally, the geographical location of Qin meant that it could fight a war only on two fronts, going east toward the Yellow River and the Central Plain or going down the Yangtze River, threatening the core lands of Chu. This prompted other states to revise their tactics and diplomacies. They realized that the Qin threat was too great for them to singlehandedly defeat themselves; thus, the century of alliances began. Two main diplomatic doctrines were the so-called vertical and horizontal alliances. The vertical alliances involved the states on the north-south axis to unitedly act against the Qin. Opposed to it was the horizontal alliance, where states allied with Qin to reap the fruits of Qin supremacy for themselves, as well as to protect their lands from Qin attacks.

But by no means does this mean that Qin was unbeatable. Though the first allied attack in 318 was a failure, the succession crisis in 307 weakened the position of Qin. This was exploited by King Min of Qi, who led an alliance attack on Qin in 298. After a few years of struggle, Qin had to yield, asking for peace, and in return, it gave portions of its western territories to Wei and Han. Continuing on that success, Qi attacked Yen and Chu as well, marking a short period of restoration of Qi power. Following some internal struggles, Qi abandoned its alliance with Wei and Han while at the same time it achieved a temporary truce with Qin. Several years later, in 288, the kings of these two states met up, and for the first time in Chinese history declared themselves di (emperors) of the west and the east, a title which was in the past preserved only for mythological semi-god rulers. This was a clear political statement for everyone about what the ultimate goal was for every king fighting in the late Warring States Period. Together, the two self-proclaimed emperors plotted to attack Zhao, but Min of Qi was persuaded by others that this would only benefit Qin at the cost of Qi supremacy. So, he backed out of the alliance and formed a new one, now aimed against Qin.

This forced the Qin ruler, Zhao, to abdicate his new title, which Min had already abandoned, and give up the territories he took from Wei and Zhao. The following year, Qi attacked and annexed Song, one of the last remaining smaller states. This kind of rise had become too alarming for other states to ignore, and in 284, Qi was simultaneously attacked by Yen, Qin, Zhao, Wei, and Han. Chou declared itself an ally of Qi, but only to retake the lands it lost around the Huai River. Qi suffered a total defeat, with the death of King Min and the destruction of all of its armies. Qi territories were occupied until 279 when they managed to regain them, but Qi was never again able to achieve its former power. But this shifting of powers and alliances was best used by the state of Zhao, which was altering its allegiance between Qi and Qin. As such, it managed to expand its territories at the expense of Wei and Qi. This expansion, coupled with military reforms, propelled Zhao to be the most powerful state in the ensuing decade, achieving several victories over Qin by 269. These defeats caused the king Zhao of Qin to change his state policies and philosophy of war.

16. Statue of a Qin soldier. Source: https://commons.wikimedia.org

His advisors pointed out to him that fighting solely for supremacy and waging war against the strongest opponent was futile, as they had seen in their experience with Qi and Zhao. So, the king of Qin decided to abandon the old system of alliances in favor of diplomacy based on a maxim "alliance with the distant and war with the neighbor." This way of thinking was aimed at achieving irreversible expansion of a state, with all new territory gains belonging solely to the king, not his generals or vassals. The sole aim of war for Qin became territorial gain. Furthermore, he stated his policy of attacking not only the lands of the enemy but people as well. This meant that the ultimate goal, besides expansion of the state, was annihilating rival armies so that enemy states would lose any capacity of fighting. But this kind of military thought wasn't developed just overnight. Over two centuries leading up to this point, armies were slowly growing from at most 30,000 at the beginning of this era to 300,000 in the last decades. Scholars today presume that these records were overexaggerated, but they clearly show an increase in the scale of warfare. With that came casualties that numbered in tens of thousands of dead and wounded.

But these high numbers of fallen soldiers aren't solely explainable by just the sheer size of the armies. Campaigns now lasted for years, not only for a single season. Soldiers were now armed with iron weapons and armor, as it became cheaper and more durable than bronze. New innovations were adapted, like the use of cavalry and crossbows, and in general, there was a substantial advance in military theory, seen in several important writings about it. At the same time, forts and defensive walls around cities became the norm, and with those, various siege techniques were developed, from traction trebuchets to digging tunnels beneath the walls. Battles and sieges became long, and all remains of feudal chivalry were lost by the mid-3rd century. This is best seen in the example of Bai Qi, a Qin general of this era who became known as Ren Tu (human butcher), who in his thirty-year career was responsible for deaths of at least 900,000 enemy soldiers. Some sources even go as high as two million, though this is likely an exaggeration. And the first to bear the Qin attack in 265 was Han, at that point the weakest surviving state and Qin's immediate neighbor. They turned to Zhao for help, which this state eagerly gave. The war dragged on in a stalemate before Qin achieved a grand victory in 260. It seemed that Qin was on the verge of final victory, but exhaustion combined with the loss of several important generals halted its expansion.

17. Qin general Bai Qi. Source: https://commons.wikimedia.org

The next step for King Zhao of Qin was a direct attack on the Zhou Dynasty in 256 BCE. No other state was able or willing to help, and with this, the Zhou lands were conquered and annexed by Qin. That is how the Zhou Dynasty finally ended. Soon afterward, King Zhao died, and after two short rules of older kings, in 247, Zhao Zheng became the new king of Qin. At the time, he was only 13 years old, so he had regents rule in his place until 235. In the first years of his rule, he was preoccupied with securing his place on the throne as he faced a rebellion, but then he started preparing his armies for one last grand campaign. The Qin military machine was finally unleashed in 230. Once again, Han was the first target. Then in 228, Zhao Zheng turned his armies against the Zhao, and in 226 he took parts of Yan. In 225, Wei fell, after which attacks were directed toward Chu, the largest remaining state. But in 223, it also fell without much resistance. The next year, Qin conquered the remaining territories of Yan in the north. And in 221, the last state to be conquered was Qi. After over two centuries of great wars, massive battles, and countless skirmishes, it took less than a decade for Zhao Zheng to achieve complete victory. He crowned his victory by assuming the emperor title huángdì, which he created himself. Thus, he became known as Qin Shi Huangdi, or the First Emperor of Qin. This marks the end of unification and the birth of imperial China.

18. Illustration of Qin Shi Huangdi from 19th century.
Source: https://commons.wikimedia.org

Ancient China had to go through rather bloody and painful labors to give birth to its first empire, but it would be unjust to speak of this period as one solely marked by wars. With constant pressures from outside and from within, Chinese states and civilization as a whole went through rather impressive advances in almost all fields. First of all, technological advances, fueled by the needs of war, were marked by an already mentioned switch to the use of iron instead of bronze. And continuing the older bronze-working traditions, the iron was also cast. This made it possible for Chinese metalsmiths to mass produce their products. This was rather important for both weapons and for various tools, as they became widespread and cheap enough for the majority to use. That led to the use of iron tools in farming, which in turn led to an increase in food production. This was also accompanied by large-scale irrigation projects, made available by increased logistics and capabilities of central governments, which also proved important for the development of agriculture. So, the Warring States Period, rather paradoxically to all of the carnage caused by such large-scale warfare, was a time of great expansion of the population. This fact is also important to explain why wars did become so massive, as there simply were more people to levy.

Yet advances didn't stop there, as the production of silk was improved which marked the beginning of what we could call the textile industry. Also, transportation was improved as carts with yokes gave way to wagons with shafts and breast harnesses, allowing horses and other tow animals to pull greater weights. At the same time, shipbuilding was also improved. And with improved production in various fields, advances in transportation, and the already mentioned implementation of money, trade also blossomed in the Warring States Period. Merchants became wealthier and held more important ranks of society, with some even managing to gain high-ranking offices in the court. Great cities and capitals were no longer just centers of political power, but also manufacturing and trading hubs.

However, not all advancements in this period were material ones. Expansion of trade pushed for improvements in applied mathematics and arithmetic. With social pressures and changes came the proliferation of philosophical thought, with the most notable being Confucianism championed by Mencius, Taoism represented by Lao Tzu, Legalism advocated by Shang Yang, and Mohism upheld by Mozi. These schools of philosophy were and still are an integral part of Chinese civilization and way of thinking and understanding the world. Advances were also made in arts, combining both material and intellectual, from the rising importance of writings, poems, and books, to stunning artisanal work from painters and sculptors. All in all, during the Warring States Period, Chinese civilization achieved an important leap forward, surpassing in a way many, if not all, contemporary cultures.

On those bases, the first Chinese empire of the Qin Dynasty was built. With unification and establishment of a new system, Qin Shi Huangdi dealt the final blow to the feudal system, as he sought only talented people to work in his purely bureaucratic administrative system, which was solely based on laws and legality and not traditions and kinship. So, instead of giving conquered lands to his family and allies, he divided the entire empire into 36 commanderies, or provinces, which were further divided into counties. These commanderies were ruled by three high-ranking officials—civil governor, military commander, and the imperial inspector, who acted as an immediate representative of the emperor. And none of these offices were hereditary. Furthermore, the emperor realized that if his rule was going to be efficient, he had to standardize all aspects of public life, like currency, measurements, the language, and the writing system, to the details such as the width of the carriage axels. With such an organized system, the Qin empire became capable enough to exercise an impressive level of control over its population, which could be seen through large-scale public works like building roads, major canals, forts, and palaces. But this is even more obvious in the two most recognizable monuments of the ancient Chinese civilization, which are admired even today. One is, of course, the Terracotta

Army, a replica of an entire army with life-sized and highly detailed soldiers, as part of the first emperor's tomb. The second one was the construction of the now world-famous Great Wall of China, as Qin Shi Huangdi ordered that the various fortifications built by states during previous periods be connected in order to protect the Qin Dynasty.

With such a powerful state government, along with a well-trained and experienced army and a booming economy, the first Chinese emperor naturally sought to expand his realm. First, in 215, he sent his general on campaigns in the north, conquering the Ordos region and parts of Inner Mongolia. With secured borders in the north, in 214, he turned his attention to the south, where he sent the majority of his armies. In a long and tough campaign against the jungle guerilla tactics of the southern tribes, his armies managed to achieve victory, pushing as far south as Hanoi, in present-day Vietnam. With those victories, Qin Shi Huang conquered and colonized large parts of the present-day provinces of Guangdong, Guangxi, and Fujian. The majority of the colonizers were actually prisoners, exiles, and poor people who were sent to assimilate the local population into Chinese civilization, to facilitate imperial rule. But despite these victories and his other administrative reforms, Qin Shi Huangdi remained rather unpopular as he was seen as a totalitarian tyrant. His punishments were cruel, and he showed little mercy. He was also criticized for murdering scholars who tried to criticize him and burned books which dealt with history and philosophies of previous eras. So, when he died in 210, not many tears were shed for him.

Commanderies (Prefectures, the Jun) of Qin Dynasty

1. Handan
2. Henei
3. Yingchuan
4. Dang
5. Xue
6. Jiaoxi
7. Linqing
8. Guangyang
9. Yunzhong

221 BC - 206 BC

19. Map of the Qin Dynasty Chinese empire.
Source: https://commons.wikimedia.org

And even worse for his legacy, right after his death, his ministers started plotting, putting his weaker and more pliable son on the throne, who became known as Qin Er Shi. His father's ministers used him as a puppet, worsening the regime. And as the new emperor lacked the authority of his father, rebellions quickly erupted both in the conquered lands and among the Qin armies. It soon proved that without proper leadership the Qin empire and its armies wouldn't be able to deal with the internal revolts. The second emperor tried to fight back, but his armies lost all battles, and finally in 207 suffered a crucial defeat in the heartland of the Qin state. At that time, his chancellor Zhao Gao decided he had no more use for him and forced him to commit suicide. This was the end of the Qin dynasty, state, and empire, although some sources say that Zhao Gao put Qin Er Shi's nephew on the throne, but as a mere king and not an emperor. In 206, a rebel named Liu Bang, who would become the founder of a new dynasty named Han, managed to conquer the Qin capital, capture the king, and gain prestige. But by that time, the entire Chinese state reverted to chaos with various rebel states and kingdoms proclaiming independence. There were still several years of war waiting for Liu Bang before he would manage to once again unite China.

Despite such a quick and rather undignified end of the Qin empire, it did represent the end product of the evolution of Chinese civilization during the Warring States Period. And despite all of the flaws of the short Qin imperial rule, it did create the basis of how the future Chinese empire would function, from highly developed administration and bureaucracy, through unified and standardized laws and measurements, and to the way the emperor himself would be seen and represented, through his sheer unquestionable authority. So, even though Qin Shi Huangdi was seen as a bad ruler, criticized for his lack of morality and his violent temper, many future emperors copied his bureaucratic system and parts of his royal ideology, making him and this period one of the most influential parts of Chinese history.

Chapter 5 – Rise and Fall of the Han Dynasty

With the fall of Qin came the rise of the first true imperial dynasty of ancient China. This dynasty took the best parts of their predecessors, building on their legacy to create a period that is widely considered to be one of China's golden ages. Under the Han rule, the economy continued to grow, culminating with the creation of the Silk Road that connected China with the Mediterranean. Technologies and science were also improving, with many inventions, like paper and ship rudders, becoming an essential stepping-stone for the advancement of the entire world. Of course, this newly found power of the Chinese empire was shown in military conquests that expanded the borders of China in pretty much every possible direction. It was indeed the age of prosperity and advancement in Chinese history. But to the contemporaries of the first Han emperor, it sure didn't seem like the future was going to be so bright.

As the revolts against the Qin rule multiplied, there was more than just one rebellion faction, but two stood out. One was led by the already mentioned Liu Bang, who was of a modest background serving as a local sheriff under the first imperial dynasty. The second was commanded by Xiang Yu, who was from a noble family, and who took over a rebellion in the former Chu state after the death of his uncle in battle. At first, Xiang Yu was more influential and successful, beating Qin armies in open battles and gaining prestige among other rebel forces. But to his dismay, Liu Bang beat him in the race over who would conquer the Qin capital and put an end to their dynasty. At that time, the two were still allies struggling against the old regime, but Xiang Yu grew restless and envious of Liu's success and prestige. But Liu remained loyal to Xiang, who, as the most powerful leader, was the de facto leader of the rebellion. It seems he doubted that the Qin government system was going to work in his favor, so he divided China into eighteen smaller kingdoms and distributed them. At this same time, Xiang Yu took the title of hegemon, as despite not being the first to the capital, he was still the strongest and most influential among the rebels. With that, he recreated the old system of the Spring and Autumn Period. In the division of lands, Xiang gave Liu Bang a small and remote fief called Hanzhong, in an attempt to remove him from the political stage. Of course, Liu felt betrayed and soon rose up to challenge the hegemony of Xiang Yu.

He first retook control of the old Qin state and from there started conquering neighboring kingdoms. An open conflict between the two leaders ensued. Success traded sides as neither faction could achieve a decisive victory or gain a considerable upper hand in the struggle. Eventually, both factions depleted their reserves and needed to recuperate, so in 203, Liu Bang and Xiang Yu agreed upon an armistice. A few months later in 202, Liu reopened hostilities, and this time he managed to achieve a complete victory at the battle of Gaixia, with the suicide of Xiang Yu being the most important gain. He was the only one capable enough to stand against Liu. And after his death, all the other kingdoms submitted to Liu, who was proclaimed the new emperor. According to Chinese tradition, his dynasty took the name of his home fief and became known as the Han Dynasty. Liu Bang himself became known as Emperor Gaozu. The new ruler of this united China chose to, in most parts, follow the laws and regulations of his Qin predecessors, though he did lower the taxes and reduced military levies to both help the population recover from the civil war and to gain the loyalty of his subjects.

But Xiang's decision to divide the Qin state into eighteen kingdoms had great repercussions to the administrative system of the early Han. In the west, covering less than half of the empire, the emperor directly controlled the territory through the commanderies, emulating the Qin bureaucratic apparatus. But the eastern parts were divided into ten vassal kingdoms, all too large and led by proven generals to be conquered easily. And this fact threatened the rule of Emperor Gaozu. So, he slowly deposed of these kings, sometimes peacefully, sometimes by a show of force, giving the crowns to his family members, as he saw administrative benefits in these kingdoms. They managed to pacify the local population and ease the toll on the central government's apparatus. By 195, only one of these kingdoms wasn't ruled by a member of the Han family. Another reason why they were useful, at least when it came to the northern borders, was that they were the first line of defense against the northern tribes, who created a confederacy among them known as Xiongnu. Gaozu tried to pacify the barbarians in 200, but was defeated, and saw that the only way out was to pay tribute to them and to give the hand of a princess to their leader. Thus, he started a diplomatic practice called heqin, by using marriage as a tool to appease too powerful neighbors.

20, Emperor Gaozu of the Han Dynasty.
Source: https://commons.wikimedia.org

But even so, the first several decades of the Han Dynasty weren't stable at all. Several vassal kings rebelled after Emperor Gaozu tried to replace them, and after a battle against one of them, he died in 195, leaving a rather weak son to succeed him. At the time, the most important person in the Chinese state became Gaozu's widow, Lü Zhi, now empress dowager. As a regent of her son, she actually pulled all the strings and started giving titles, offices, and other government positions to members of her own clan. This antagonized other members of the Han family, but she remained in power until her death in 180. Under her watchful eye, three emperors changed on the throne, two of them being her grandsons, yet none proved to be able to pull away from her influence. Indeed, just before her death, one of the vassal kings from the Han family was ready to start another civil war, while the northern tribes once again raided the Chinese territories. But without her leadership, opposition to the Han kings was almost nonexistent, and their coup caused little disturbance as the Lü clan had little support. They also deposed the fourth emperor of the Han dynasty as he was seen only as the Lü clan's puppet, and the question arose who would inherit the imperial throne. Instead of looking at seniority, three Han kings chose the most suitable candidate between them, picking Liu Heng, Gaozu's son, as the most virtuous. Thus, he became Emperor Wen.

Rather quickly, it became obvious he was a good choice, as his policies were benevolent and aimed at bettering the lives of his subjects. He lowered taxes, created government aid for people in need, and made punishments for breaking the law less harsh. Under his rule, Taoist liberal teachings permeated the ideology of the central government. Emperor Wen also recognized the threat of the Xiongnu confederation, once again using the heqin policy to achieve peace on the northern borders. But he was also wise enough to realize that large kingdoms were a constant internal threat, so he used occasions when kings died without an heir to reduce the sizes of the kingdoms, without causing many revolts among his vassals. His peaceful and successful reign, which lasted until 157, was exactly what the Han Dynasty needed to stabilize their place on the throne. The effects of his reign were further expanded by the peaceful succession and rule of his son, Emperor Jing. He continued his father's policies, further cutting down on taxes and criminal punishments. He also continued his father's policy of reducing kingdoms, which finally prompted a failed rebellion of seven kingdoms in 154. After Emperor Jing's victory, the authority and power of the vassal kingdoms ensued, as well as the creation of new commanderies.

The end result of these administrative changes carried out by the two emperors can be seen in the fact that in 179 there were 19 commanderies and 11 relatively large kingdoms. By 143, there were 40 commanderies and 25 smaller kingdoms, significantly increasing the authority of the central government. Emperor Jing died in 141, leaving a stable and rather wealthy empire to his son, Emperor Wu (sometimes called Wudi). The first several years of his lengthy reign were marked by a series of reforms, as the new emperor saw flaws in the Taoist ideology and in the overdependency of the noble class, which grew strong under the rule of Wen and Jing. Despite some early opposition to his plans, Wu managed to go through with them. He reinstituted the meritocratic system in the government bureaucracy, leaving room for talented individuals of lower classes who were taught in Confucian and traditionalist thoughts. He also continued administrative changes of his predecessors, reducing the size of both the kingdoms and commanderies, thus further limiting the power of local nobles. Emperor Wu also created a position of regional inspectors, who were given a large area in which they represented the emperor and kept kings, governors, and other officials in check. This was an attempt to limit corruption and raise the efficiency of the government system.

21. Later portrait of Emperor Wu. Source:
https://commons.wikimedia.org

Emperor Wu changed economic policies, abolishing the loose
Taoist principles used before and adding and raising taxes. He
also sought to mint money and to control mining and salt
production through the state, as monopolies on those industries
gave more power and wealth to the state. His government also
sought to organize other parts of economic life, like trade,
transportation, and prices. Wu also realized that agriculture was
the main driving force of China's economy, so his government
tried to stimulate it, without too many regulations, which led to the
creation of a large landowner class. This was objected by some, as
it led to a further rise in inequality, but he cared little about that;
he needed to raise income to his treasury to fuel his campaigns
and conquests. He aimed at expanding his empire in two main
directions. First was to the south and southwest, conquering the

Nanyue and Minyue kingdoms. This was in a way a replication of Qin campaigns, but with more permanent results, as the regions from modern-day Fujian to northern Vietnam and the eastern parts of Yenan came under the control of the Chinese empire. Roughly at the same time, Emperor Wu realized that the Xiongnu were too much of a threat, so the second direction of his campaigns was to the north and northwest.

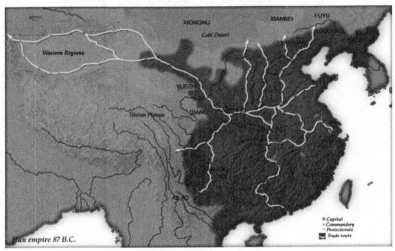

22. Han empire in 87 BCE. Source: https://commons.wikimedia.org

The Chinese armies were successful there as well, driving off the northern barbarians and expanding their territories. But due to the reports of his subordinates, who told him about the importance of trade with faraway countries which were as rich as China, Emperor Wu decided to push his conquest farther in the west, into the Gobi Desert and Central Asia. These conquests helped the establishment of the Silk Road, a trade route which connected China with the Parthian Empire and the Mediterranean, and facilitated commerce along it. The majority of these conquests were achieved between 138 and 110, though fighting against the Xiongnu continued in later decades as well. In the ending years of the 2nd century BCE, Chinese forces also managed to conquer northern parts of the Korean Peninsula, which marked the end of Emperor Wu's expansion politics. Although he achieved vast territorial expansion, it was a rather costly venture in both human lives and money. Thus, in the later years of his reign, he focused on securing his conquests and stabilizing the internal affairs of his empire. It was clear that the burden of war fell heavy on the people, but more importantly, dynastic disputes slowly arose, culminating with the revolt of Wu's son and heir, Prince Ju, in 91/90. As a result, Wu left his throne to his youngest son, who was only 6 years old when the emperor died in 87 after ruling for 54 years, a record that wasn't broken by another Chinese emperor for another 1,800 years.

In the end, the rule of Emperor Wu was seen as a mixture of bad and good. He did raise the taxes and burden his people with long warfare, and despite his proclamations of Confucianism, he based his administrative system more on Qin legalism, ruling similarly to the first emperor. On the other hand, he did expand China into territories that to this day are part of the country, and he also furthered international trade and managed to strengthen the authority of the central government. Whether he's seen as a good or bad ruler, the fact remains that he propelled Han China to the level of a world power. But after his death came two less abled emperors, who remained under a strong influence of their regent, Huo Guang. The first of them, Wu's youngest son, died of natural causes in 74, and the other was deposed by Huo, as he was declared unfit to rule that very same year. Huo then chose Emperor Xuan for the throne, continuing to play an important role in the state until his death in 68. Those twenty odd years he was in charge he spent lowering the taxes and burdens on the people, and continued the expansion of the empire in Central Asia, but retained strict, almost despotic, rule. And as such, later historians gave him credit for being a capable administrator who acted in the best interest of the dynasty, but who overstepped his authority and ruled rather harshly.

But his death and the purging of his entire clan from the state administration in 66, changed the course of Chinese politics. Emperor Xuan further cut state spending by stopping all military campaigns and turning to diplomacy and colonization to protect the gained territories. He also refrained from an extravagant lifestyle, devoting himself to ruling as best as he could and promoting Confucianism as the state ideology. But slowly, administrative officers started to gain power, as the emperor lacked a firm hand to subdue their desires. This trend continued and even worsened after his death in 49, under the reign of his son, Emperor Yuan. Factionalism appeared among the officials, with various groups fighting for supremacy, which made the central government weaker. During Yuan's rule, some of the old kingdoms were resurrected, though for a short period, while laws became less harsh and economic control of the state lessened, though some attempts to break up lands of large landowners were made to make Chinese society more egalitarian. But in the end, that failed. And in foreign policies, he was peaceful, like his father, though some fighting occurred as the northern barbarians became restless once again. The Chinese state, together with its emperors, were growing mellow, even abandoning some of the conquered lands.

The state of the Han Dynasty worsened with Yuan's son, Cheng. He ascended to the throne in 33, and his interests lay with chasing women and enjoying life rather than ruling the empire. While he ruled, the clan Wang started to grow in power and influence in the royal court, as this was the family of Grand Empress Dowager Wang, wife of Emperor Yuan. She used her longevity and influence, exploiting the weaknesses of her son to promote her family members into vital positions in the empire. One after another, members of the Wang clan were given the high command of the entire Chinese army, and eventually, in 8 BCE, this position was given to Wang Mang. A year later, Emperor Cheng died childless, so his nephew, Ai, became the new emperor. At first, the young emperor tried to rule on his own, reducing spending, limiting slavery, and trying to force out the Wang clan from their offices. He managed to strip Wang Mang, but Grand Empress Dowager Wang was still in court, plotting. At the time, Ai got rather connected to a minor official named Dong Xian, promoting him rather quickly to higher ranks. This caused rumors of a supposed homosexual relationship, which was furthered by the fact that childless Ai wanted to leave his throne to Dong. Thus, another succession crisis emerged in 1 BCE when Ai died. Dong Xian and his entire family were forced to commit suicide, and another one of Cheng's nephews was chosen to be emperor. Wang Mang became his regent as the emperor was still a child.

23. Illustration of Emperor Ai and Dong Xian.
Source: https://commons.wikimedia.org

But the child emperor died in 6 CE, and an underage cousin related to Emperor Xuan became the emperor, once again under Wang Mang's regency. The remaining members of the Han family were by now already irritated by the power of Wang Mang and his attitude toward them. To please them, he promised that he would relinquish all power to the young emperor when he became old enough. But in 9 CE, he dethroned him, proclaiming that the Han Dynasty lost its Mandate of Heaven, and created a new Xia Dynasty, bringing the first era of the Han to an end. By that time, Mang had full control of the royal government and forces, so he managed to quickly put down two rebellions and a mutiny that sprang up as a reaction to his usurpation of the throne. He then had to fight off raids by the Xiongnu, who once again became restless. Through war and diplomacy, he managed to once again secure peace with them by 19 CE. He also had troubles with southwestern tribes and on the Korean Peninsula, but these revolts were caused by the earlier Han reign, not himself. And once on the throne, he reformed the Chinese economy once again by monopolizing salt and iron production, monetary reforms, as well as raising old and imposing new taxes. Wang instituted an income tax for professionals and skilled laborers and a "sloth tax" for landowners if they left their field uncultivated. In essence, these economic reforms were used to once again strengthen the imperial power and gather funds to keep the government afloat.

These reforms were later seen as a sign of Wang Mang being a despotic tyrant, but in reality, he was a capable leader who ruled with great diligence, doing nothing that many emperors before him hadn't done. He even punished his own sons when they broke the law. Yet, because his attempts to start a new dynasty failed, he has been labeled as an evil emperor, and his actions were seen as the cause for his downfall. But the fact was that the Yellow River flooded twice under his rule, changing course, and causing massive famine, migrations, and general chaos in the Chinese heartland. Wang Mang tried to fix the problems, but natural disasters of that level were something that no Chinese government, not even in the 20th century, could deal with. In the end, peasant uprisings broke out in the former Qi state in 22 CE, defeating the imperial army, and then spreading farther through China. This was a perfect opportunity for the remnants of the Han Dynasty to arise, combining their forces with the peasant's, starting a full-out civil war. By the next year, Wang Mang was overwhelmed and defeated in his capital, dying in the process. The winning force proclaimed Emperor Gengshi the new leader, as he was a descendant of Emperor Jing. But he was a weak ruler not recognized by all of the rebel forces, so the civil war continued.

After a series of bad decisions, in 25 CE, Gengshi was killed, and another descendant of Emperor Jing became the new ruler of China. Emperor Guangwu was the one who actually restored the Han Dynasty. The new emperor moved his capital from Chang'an to a city called Luoyang. Because of that move, this change in the ruling branch of the Han Dynasty causes historians to divide its history into the Western Han and Eastern Han eras. But the civil war wasn't over yet. Peasants were still unsatisfied, their army roaming the Chinese heartland, and there were at least eleven other pretenders to the throne. For more than a decade, Guangwu had to fight all of them before he could confirm his position and bring much-needed peace in 36 CE. He then proceeded to rule with frugality, with the effective and efficient government once again based on capable people. He also restored the administrative division on commanderies and small kingdoms, which he gave to his family members. Guangwu also relaxed formerly strict laws, making his reign easier and more bearable for his subjects. Under his reign, he also had to deal with smaller Xiongnu raids in the northern borders as well as a rebellion in the southern regions, in what is today North Vietnam. He also waged a campaign that restored Chinese influence in Central Asia. Ruling until 57 CE, he gave the Chinese empire much-needed stability.

He was succeeded by his son, Emperor Ming. He was strict with his officials, whom he punished severely if they were reported for abuse of their power. That made the atmosphere in his imperial court rather tense, with many political plays and backstabbing among the officials. He was extremely harsh when his brothers tried to plot against him, in one case even massacring thousands of people trying to find out all the culprits. But despite that, his reign is remembered as a positive one, with many public projects that benefited economic development. Chief among them was the repair of canals, dikes, and parts of water infrastructure that was destroyed in the massive floodings of the Yellow River at the beginning of the century. In the later years of his rule, he also waged war against some Xiongnu tribes to reaffirm China's sovereignty of the Central Asian vassal kingdoms. He died in 75 CE, succeeded peacefully by his son, Emperor Zhang. He continued in his father's footsteps, working diligently and living thriftily. He sought honest and hardworking men to appoint to his government and tried to expand trade, making it easier by developing new trade routes. And like his father, he tried to stay humble by following the Confucian teachings until his death in 88. Their reigns are often considered the second golden age of the Han Dynasty, marked by a rise in prosperity, technological advances, and overall peace.

24. A tomb mural of Chinese chariots and cavalry.
Source: https://commons.wikimedia.org

One of the reasons for this kind of stability was the ability of the first three Eastern Han emperors to keep their courts relatively free of intrigue, limiting the meddling of their wives' clans, other influential officials, and eunuchs, whose role in court life started to rise. But with the new emperor, He, being a child, the empire started to revert back to the state of the late Western Han Dynasty. The Dou clan of his mother held a tight grip on the court, but thanks to his brother, Prince Xiao, and one of the eunuchs from the court, he managed to topple them and continue his rule on his own, while also relying on the advice of capable officials around him, as he lacked the capabilities of his father and grandfather. But he did provide relief in times of crisis and tried to govern as a righteous ruler. During his time, China lost control over Central Asia and had to put up with some minor rebellions in the southwestern regions. He died in 106 without a proper heir, so after some court intrigues, Prince Xiao's son inherited the throne as Emperor An. He was also only a child, so another empress dowager ruled as his regent, promoting her own Dang clanmates into vital government positions. This changed in 121 with the death of the empress dowager.

With the help of his wife, Empress Yan, and some eunuchs deposed by the Dang clan, the vacuum in power was filled by the Yan clan and the eunuchs themselves. Under An's rule, the rebellion of the Qiang people in the southwest worsened, causing further stress in the imperial budget that had already suffered depletion dealing with the natural disasters that struck China under his rule. In 124, he died, without managing to prove any worth as an emperor. Once again, a succession crisis struck imperial China, as Empress Yan tried to instate a younger prince as a ruler to exert more power in future years, but was opposed by eunuchs who themselves sought influence over the new emperor. After a series of struggles and one short rule of Emperor Shao, the empress and her clan lost the struggle. They were slaughtered, with the exception of the empress herself, and in 125, Emperor Shun came to the throne. But nothing important changed in the imperial court, as Shun was also shown to have no strength or authority, relying on corrupt eunuchs to rule.

Despite that, his reign managed to pass without too much turmoil, mostly due to his kind nature and careful choice of the empress to avoid further treachery in court. Regardless, the government was becoming ever more corrupt on all levels, making his rule less effective. However, the central imperial government under Emperor Shun worked on many local projects and once again supported the development of education and science, as seen in his restoration of the Imperial University, which had decayed over the decades. His rule is also notable for the first use of a seismograph in history, an instrument which helps detect earthquakes. And during this period, Chinese generals were also able for a short period to restore imperial influence in Central Asia, but by that time, it was clear that the power of the empire was slowly fading. Emperor Shun died in 144, leaving his one-year-old son on the throne, but he died the very next year. And here, once again, an empress dowager started exerting great influence, despite Shun's attempts to stop that. She chose another underaged heir, a great-grandson of Emperor Zhang, who was poisoned in 146 by the empress dowager's brother, Liang Ji. Next to be chosen as emperor was another great-grandson of Emperor Zhang, Emperor Huan. In the early years of his rule, Liang Ji's influence in the court grew, becoming more powerful than his sister. But Huan wasn't eager to remain their puppet, so he turned to another evil for help, to the ever-stronger court eunuchs.

In 159, they managed to stage a coup, and the Liang clan was slaughtered and all their supporters in the government purged. People expected that the situation in the empire would change, but because Emperor Huan had to rely on eunuchs to achieve this, he rewarded them with government positions, money, and power. Thus, his rule remained overshadowed by others. But he himself was a corrupt ruler, who disregarded all criticism and advice of his capable administrators, which worsened the situation. This was reflected in the numerous peasant revolts across the Chinese empire, as well as the renewed rebellion of the Qiang people in the southwest. Quelling these drained the imperial treasury, and in 161, Huan set a disastrous precedent of selling minor government positions and offices for money. Seeing how eunuchs became too powerful, several Confucian scholars that served in the central government, supported by the students of the Imperial University, tried to suppress their influence. This evolved into an open student protest in 166, which angered the emperor. He imprisoned many of them, thus turning scholars to another opposition to the throne and further alienating the people the empire needed the most, capable and educated ones. The rule of Emperor Huan ended in 168, and he died without a son.

Once again, a crucial role was played an empress dowager, Dou, who picked another child emperor descended from one of Emperor Zhao's sons. He was called Ling, and like his predecessors, he was controlled by the empress dowager's regency. Dou tried to limit the power of the eunuchs, but in the end, it backfired on her. In 169, they seized her, slaughtered her clan, and took over control of the emperor. The corruption and selling of offices and titles continued, while the eunuchs continued to plot and gain more power in the court. Taxes were raised as the imperial treasury began to dry out due to the corrupt bureaucracy. On top of all that, the Chinese army suffered a terrible defeat in 177 from the Xianbei, a new barbarian confederation in the north. All this led to a peasant revolt in central China in 184 known as the Yellow Turban Rebellion, led by a Taoist preacher who claimed that the era of the Han Dynasty was over. Despite its religious background, it was an organized attempt to seize the throne, and the central government had to send several armies to quell it. In the end, its leader was killed, and it slowly started to disband. Yet agrarian revolts, rebellions, and other uprisings continued as the state of the empire continued to decay.

The Yellow Turban Rebellion managed to cause substantial unrest, but its more important result was that for the first time generals didn't disband their armies after the imperial victory, as they sensed they would need it again soon. The rebellion also caused some court officials to persuade Emperor Ling that imperial inspectors didn't have enough power. Thus, in 188, he gave them the authority to command imperial troops and raise taxes in their regions, changing their titles to governors. Many high-ranking officials and generals were granted this new title and power, enabling them in just a few years to grow into local warlords. The very next year Liang died. His older son became the new emperor, but court intrigues continued, and after less than two weeks, he was deposed and soon after killed. Liang's other son became the next and last Han emperor. The very beginning of his rule was filled with the usual court games of the eunuchs, but this time they bit off more than they could chew, as their treachery was discovered by one of the high-ranking officers. After some political machinations, he attacked them and then executed them in 189. With that, any remaining power of the central imperial government was lost, and warlords started to arise.

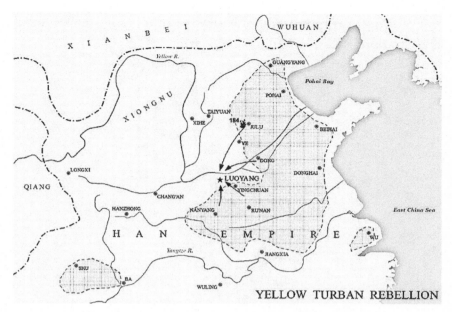

25. Map showing the extent of the Yellow Turban Rebellion.
Source: https://commons.wikimedia.org

One of them, Dong Zhuo, seized this opportunity and took control of the emperor and the central government, calling himself chancellor of the state. Soon other warlords rose up against him, followed by peasant uprisings. This weakened his position, and in 192, he was assassinated in a court plot. After his death, most people hoped that the Han regime would return to its normal state, but the inertia of the civil war forced warlords to continue their fights as they feared retribution. Thus, the warfare continued while the imperial court lost not only its power but its source of income, with members of the central government literally dying from hunger. Emperor Xian couldn't find anyone to help him until 196 when a warlord named Cao Cao invited the emperor and his court to him. Until this period, he was only a minor warlord, but he recognized the benefits of having control of the emperor, despite his total lack of authority. He quickly gained influence, becoming one of the more important warlords in a matter of years by conquering smaller states around him. By the end of the 2nd century, China was divided into many smaller and larger warlord states, locked in all-out civil war.

26. Last Han Dynasty emperor Xian on the left and warlord Cao Cao on the right. Source: https://commons.wikimedia.org

At first, Cao Cao preserved the emperor's central government as it was, with all its ministers and officials. But in 208, he abolished all imperial offices, replacing them with only two, the imperial secretary and the chancellor, a title he took for himself. With that, the imperial authority of Emperor Xian was destroyed, and he became a mere puppet, similar to the earlier Zhou kings during the Spring and Autumn Period. In those early years of the 3rd century, beside Cao Cao in the north, two more warlords rose to the top, making it, in essence, a three-way fight for the throne. One was Liu Bei in the southwest, a possible distant member of a Han family, and Sun Quan in the southeast. By 220, Cao Cao died, and he was succeeded by his son Cao Pi, who shared the ambitions of his father. By the end of that very same year, he managed to force Emperor Xian to abdicate in his favor, as Cao Pi wanted to prove his power. With that act, the Han Dynasty ended after ruling China for more than 400 years. Xian wasn't killed; instead, he continued to live a rather luxurious life as a duke on a fief given to him by Pi. The other two warlords didn't wait long to raise their titles as well. Liu Bei took the title of an emperor in 221, while Sun Quan followed them both taking the same title in 229. Thus, China was divided into three states, Wei, Shu, and Wu, and the period of the Three Kingdoms began.

But despite this rather inglorious end, the Han Dynasty has been widely regarded as one of the golden ages of China. And rightfully so. Looking just on the surface, China vastly expanded its territory, from Korea to Vietnam and far into Central Asia, all the way up to present-day Kazakhstan. The economy also blossomed, both from the rise in the production of silk, iron, and ceramics, as well as because of trade. One of their most important contributions was the Silk Road that connected China to Europe. But under the Han Dynasty, Chinese culture also developed from many important philosophers and books that are still preserved today. But also, it was a period of numerous technological and scientific breakthroughs as well as developments of art. Thus, this period became a classical period of Chinese history, rather influential and regarded in ensuing generations of Chinese thinkers. And so, it was the Han who actually molded traditions of previous dynasties with their own unique attributions to create a basis of quintessential features of Chinese civilization.

Chapter 6 – Society of Ancient China

China went through enormous changes in every aspect of life during ancient times. From the time of early Shang to the late Han, China's social order, economy, bureaucracy, and even the everyday life developed, modified, and transformed. The society of the Shang is vastly different from the society of the Han, yet in this chapter, we shall try to explain some of the basic trends, characteristics, and evolution of the ancient Chinese society, but focusing more on the later Han Dynasty, as it was the period of its most complex state covered by this guide.

On top of the Chinese social hierarchy was its sovereign, and that stayed the same from the earliest days of Chinese civilization until the end of the Han Dynasty. But their titles, importance, and authority did change. The earliest historical sovereigns, not including mythical emperors, carried the titles of kings (wang), and like in most primitive early societies their rule was based on dual authority. One was their religious role, as during the Shang Dynasty and even in the early Zhou, they were vital for carrying out various rituals and ceremonies. The other was their material power, seen through simple wealth and the ability to command human resources of the commoners, both for war and for building projects. But over time, their authority grew until they were able to exert a much higher level of control over their subjects, who grew in numbers. Thus, during the Zhou Dynasty, they started to abandon their religious roles, leaving them to the priests, and focused more on developing their political and governmental functions. But during the later Zhou period, their actual authority had diminished, and they became rather insignificant. But as their nominally subordinated dukes became kings as well during the Warring States Period, their different philosophies of rule caused a change in the role of the sovereign.

Rulers of that period realized that they needed to further their own prerogatives and share less of their power with the nobles, increasing their authority. Thus, when the king of Qin became the first emperor, he took for himself absolute power. He was the only one who could issue and modify laws, as he was the supreme judge and commander-in-chief. No one could dispute his decisions, and he had the power to interfere with anyone's life. And with few exceptions, all the lands belonged to him. His ceremonial roles were almost all gone, yet there still remained a religious link between imperial authority and religion, and this was the idea of the Mandate of Heaven. First introduced by the Zhou kings, it gave the Chinese sovereigns theological legitimacy, as their authority was given and confirmed by heaven. This was especially important in periods of dynastic change, as in theory, it gave everyone the right to rebel against the emperor if his rule showed great signs of misfortune. But at the same time, it made imperial rule mostly unquestionable, making any revolts counter to the natural order of the universe. And in a way, the emperor himself equaled the state. But this dominating role of Chinese emperors was theoretical, as we have seen that their authority was often usurped by others when persons on the throne were weak.

Of course, none of the sovereigns, no matter their titles, could rule on their own. They had their officials and administrations beneath them. In the early days, the court was filled with feudal nobles, who had their own land and rights to do as they please with them. They only served the king by paying tributes and waging wars when asked. Other than that, royal authority exerted little power in the feudal states. To combat that over the centuries, the Chinese sovereigns worked on revoking feudal titles, creating a bureaucratic government. This process was finalized with the establishment of the empire in 221 BCE, but the Han Dynasty introduced an exception. Semi-autonomous fiefs were reestablished but only for members of the royal family, and their power was constantly kept in check. This, in turn, meant that pretty much all nobles were in some way connected with the imperial family. Of course, this didn't mean that other noble families disappeared. They transformed into a new class of educated gentry that served in the imperial administration. The core of the central government were positions of three excellences, whose exact titles vary. But they were the emperor's closest advisors, whose jurisdictions were separated in three often not strictly divided areas of government. Below them were nine ministers, each with their own distinct sectors, like a minister of finance or justice. They were responsible for carrying out the emperor's orders and taking care of everyday state bureaucracy.

27. Han period figurine of two scholarly gentry men playing a board game. Source: https://commons.wikimedia.org

The greatest distinction between the nobles and officials is in the fact that noble titles were hereditary, but officials were appointed by the emperor. This made vertical social mobility in the Chinese society greater than most other ancient states. In theory, anyone capable could progress, but of course, wealthier people were at an advantage. For one, they had access to better education, and also their connections, which remained an important function in Chinese society, were greater, allowing them to advance faster and higher than commoners. Yet that division between the elites and the commoners was something that changed over time. In the early days, Chinese society was clearly divided into two main groups, the feudal elite and the peasant commoners. But as Chinese civilization grew more complex, the society went through stratification based on wealth and occupation. So, during the Han Dynasty, just below the nobles and officials were rich merchants, landowners, and industrialists, with the latter sometimes being outlawed by the nationalization of the industries. Landowners most often weren't working on their land, but rented it to tenants or hired a workforce to farm the lands for them while they lived in cities. Industrialists were people who dealt in the mining of metals, salt extraction, large-scale manufacturing, or animal breeding. They often owned compatible businesses, like iron mines and iron workshops, magnifying their profit in the process. And finally, there were itinerant merchants that traded with valuable commodities in a network of cities across China. It should be mentioned that often these three social groups mixed, as a single person could trade goods he manufactured while he owned large land parcels.

Below them were craftsman and artisans who created specialized articles like weapons, jewelry, and other more artistic products. Their status was solely dependent on their abilities in their craft. Some of them became rich and respected members of society, while others were measly workers without much class. Yet in the social hierarchy, they were seen as being above the local traders and small merchants, who were often despised by the gentry and sometimes even persecuted by the law, being forced to wear clothes that signified their status. An exception to this rule were booksellers and apothecaries which were seen as worthy professions by the scholarly gentry and which they sometimes engaged with. Then came the farmers and peasants, who worked on their lands. Farmers and peasants are often seen as a higher class than the artisans due to Confucian thought as they produced all the food that society depended on. This was also the only manual labor that was respected by the elites, as it was seen as something decent and humble. But of course, almost none of them worked on their own fields. Farmers had to work hard on their fields, many of them owning the lands they worked on. Others were simply tenant farmers, working on lands that they rented from the elite landowners. As they represented about 90% of the Chinese population, they were actually the base of the entire economy, so when natural disaster threatened them, the economy in whole was in danger. That is why the central government took great care to preserve this class. They were also important as they were the base for conscription, both for military service and for corvée labor, which is unpaid work owed by a subject to his feudal lord. Other lower classes were subject to this as well, but they were less numerous, thus less important.

A separate social group was that of retainers or clients, which started to form in large numbers during the Warring States Period. These were people without their own lands or possessions who lived at their hosts, providing labor for lodging, food, and in some cases wages. Two types of retainers could be distinguished. The lower and lesser respected were those who provided manual labor around the house and estate. Then there were those who served as bodyguards and combatants, who in later periods of the Han Dynasty grew into personal armies. The most notable and respected were those in advisory and scholarly roles. Some of the retainers who performed well for their hosts were even gifted luxurious items, which served to show how respected they could become.

28. Han ceramic figurines of servants.
Source: https://commons.wikimedia.org

Contrary to them were the slaves who were, of course, the lowest layer of Chinese society. They themselves were the property of their owners, and they could be split into two major groups, state and private slaves. The two most common ways to become a slave was through debt or as a prisoner of war. Yet it should be noted that slaves weren't a substantial part of Chinese society, making maybe 1% of the entire population. They never played a crucial role in the Chinese economy or way of life, and in some occasions during the Han rule, slavery was shortly abolished as it was seen as a rather immoral practice. Also, slaves were protected by the law, preventing their owners from murdering them, even in the case of vassal kings or other lesser nobilities. But children of slaves were born as slaves.

But beside this vertical division of the Chinese society into broad classes, there was also a form of horizontal division into clans, as family played an important role in the life of the Chinese. Of course, the core of these clans was the patrilineal nuclear family in which the father was the head of the family. During the Han Dynasty, it was rare to see generations of one family living under one roof. But they remained connected with their relatives with whom they shared a common patrilineal ancestor. Of course, the closer they were related, the stronger the bond. But it was common for clan members to look out for their fellow kinsmen, which in turn caused plenty of problems for the central government. The most common reason was that officials on all levels often promoted and helped their clan members, which caused those lineages to grow in power, and from time to time even threaten the imperial authority. It was also a fertile ground for corruption and nepotism in administration. Local clans were also often backbones of rebellions and revolts. And there was nothing that the government could do against the institution of the kin as it was rooted in Confucian traditions.

29. Two frescoes of noble Han women.
Source: https://commons.wikimedia.org

Marriage itself was seen as part of this kinship system, as often marriages were arranged or influenced by the family head, not solely based on choices of the newlyweds. But matrilineal relatives were not considered members of the clan, and when the wife would enter a new family, she became part of the husband's clan, worshiping in his familial temple. However, she retained her natal surname. Monogamy was the norm in Chinese society, with exceptions being very wealthy nobles and imperial family. These men had one chief wife and then numbers of concubines, who legally and religiously had lesser rights. Tradition called for all women to obey their husbands and other male family members, and it was common for the mother of the clan leader to retain seniority. This was most obvious in the imperial court where empress dowagers often played crucial roles, having more authority than the emperors themselves. There were other cases when women managed to gain influence and were involved with jobs not traditionally considered suitable for them. But most of them were tasked with domestic duties, such as weaving clothes, cooking, and taking care of children. In rare occasions they worked in the fields alongside the male members of their families or wove silk or other more exclusive textiles for extra income. This was more common for widows. Divorce also existed but was frowned upon as immoral. Mostly this right was reserved for husbands, who could request it if the wife was disobedient, unfaithful, or infertile. Women could in some rare cases ask for a divorce if the husband's family couldn't materially provide for her.

Women also had some protection by the law. For one, they were excluded from corvée labor, and by the Han times, husbands were forbidden to physically abuse their wives. Rape was also banned, and women could sue their attackers in court. These, like most of the imperial laws, trace their origins to the earlier archaic forms based on customs and natural law, which matured by the time of the Han Dynasty. For example, Han legislation distinguished different types of murder, differentiating killing with intent from accidental murder. And the imperial law dealt with a wide array of offenses and obligations, outlining various forms of punishments. According to some sources, one of the early Han codices of law had 26,000 articles. Interestingly, incarceration wasn't common in Chinese law. Death sentences, usually by beheading, periods of forced hard labor, exile, and monetary fines were the usual punishments. And like most legal systems, the imperial Chinese judiciary system had several levels, from the county court, headed by a county magistrate, going up with the administrative levels of the government. In cases where jurisdiction overlapped, it was common that whoever arrested the criminal would be the first to judge the criminal.

But despite this level of development of the law system, trade remained mostly regulated by customs and personal agreements. It was a common practice in the Han period to have a contract, detailing the goods, amounts of money and dates, and other details. This was very important as it made trade more secure, further improving the economy. The first type of trade to develop was local trade, which grew into regional during the Zhou Dynasty. And after the creation of the empire, this evolved into domestic trade that covered the entire Chinese territory. Three types of goods were commonly sold, probably the most important of these being basic types of food—various types of millet, rice, wheat, beans, apricots, plums, peaches, chickens, pigs, beef, and many others. Then came the everyday commodities like oil lamps, various iron and bronze farming tools and weapons, clothing, eating utensils, ceramic wares, pottery, coffins, and even carts. In the same economic category as everyday commodities were consumables like liquor, dried fish, various sauces and relishes, spices, pickles, and similar products. The third major group consisted of raw materials like jade, metal ores, salt, hide, timber, and bamboo. A wide array of tradeable goods meant that the trade network was rather developed and important, not only for the economy but also the overall quality of life in ancient China.

But even more important than domestic trade was foreign trade, which flourished with the forming of the Silk Road in the 2nd century BCE. Before that, the main trading partners of Chinese merchants were northern barbarian tribes which offered horses and fur for food and luxurious items, most commonly silk. But with the Silk Road came more prosperous trading partners, most notably Parthians (Persians) and Romans, who themselves had rich and powerful empires. And as these were long distances, covered either by land through Central Asia to present-day Iran or by maritime routes from Vietnam across the Indian subcontinent to Persian Gulf shores, this meant the only goods traded were expensive, luxurious items. From China came silk, a highly sought after good by the Romans, but also ceramics, jade and bronze items, spices, lacquerware, and others. In turn, the Chinese imported products like gold and silver, sugar, horses, and glassware. But as the silk production was at the time a technology possessed solely by the Chinese, their economy profited more from this trade, which could in part explain the booming economy of the Han Dynasty. It is also a reminder that despite the general notion that Chinese civilization developed in an isolated bubble, it actually had connections with other nations and people around them. Though the question of direct contact between the Romans and the Chinese is still debated among historians, it is evident that the exchange of knowledge and ideas did happen.

And knowledge was seen as rather important in China, especially since the transition from feudal into a bureaucratic state system began. Gathering and sharing knowledge and experience became paramount for creating capable administrators and other officials. Thus, education started playing a rather important role in Chinese society, at least among the higher classes, which is why feudal nobles transformed into a class of scholarly gentry. There were several ways to gain an education in ancient China. There were private schools opened by teachers where they taught their students for hefty tuition fees. In some cases, rich families paid teachers to educate their heirs. From those beginnings, public education began as administration grew more complex under the imperial rule. So, on a local level, schools were sponsored by commandery governments. Most of the students attending these schools remained in local lower administration offices. More prestigious was the Imperial University in the capital, which gathered the best talents across the nation and who could only enroll based on the recommendation of higher officers. Their education was directly overseen by one of the ministers, and they were prepared for high-ranking offices in the central government. The most common topics taught were philosophy, mostly Confucianism, law, mathematics, and writing. But despite the overall importance of education for the government, it was available almost exclusively to the wealthier young males, while the poor and women were usually excluded.

From this brief introduction and description of ancient Chinese society, it should become quite clear that by the time of the Han Dynasty it became very complex. From a simple two-layered society, it grew into a system of numerous classes and vocations, with very diverse stratification. Also, clans and familial ties played an important role in pinpointing one's place in society, as well as gender. But it was a very organized and regulated system, and in many ways, it is comparable with the complexity of modern societies, with many nuances and exceptions.

Chapter 7 – The Ancient Chinese Culture

The culture of the ancient Chinese came from a very humble beginning, in a way falling behind the Egyptians, Mesopotamians, and even Hindus. But since the Shang Dynasty, it started to develop at a very quick pace and in a unique way as at the time China didn't have many connections with other civilizations. From there it became one of the most important cultures in world history, influencing much of Asia as well as the rest of the world. Thanks to that, Chinese culture is today considered by many as one of the most influential and important cultures. And it is still standing on foundations and ways of thinking set in those ancient times.

In most early civilizations, the first forms of cultural development came through religion. And in turn, religion influenced further creations in intellectual and artistic forms of culture. The Chinese were no exception in this, as shamanism and naturalistic religion were the first things that formed in the pre-dynastic times, which is today called Chinese folk religion. Their core beliefs lay in veneration of nature and balance, worshiping deities, spirits, and ancestors, as well as practicing divination and exorcism. It was based on various mythological stories and traditions, like the one retold at the beginning of this guide about the creation of the world. Exact details of these myths changed over time and also varied based on location, but a similar core remained. Beliefs were, and to some extent still are, expressed through various ceremonies, in both public and private familial temples and shrines. Yet there wasn't a unified church institution, though early kings were seen as the supreme shamans. Some of the basic concepts are the well-known yin and yang, which is the balance of light and dark, idealizing harmony and natural order. They also believed in Heaven, as seen in the Mandate of Heaven doctrine, but also in natural life, known as qi (or chi). They had numerous gods and immortals but also believed in ghosts and demons. As Chinese civilization evolved, this folk religion lost its vital importance but remained an ever-present part of everyday life of the commoners even in modern times. It also influenced later developments of philosophical thoughts in ideas of harmony or respecting ancestors and elders.

From this religious background came the golden age of Chinese philosophy in the late Spring and Autumn and early Warring States Periods. This movement became known as the Hundred Schools of Thought because of the sheer number of new schools, teachings, and philosophies. Among them, and probably the most important and influential, was Confucianism, named after its founder Confucius (551–479 BCE). It was based on idealized views of the religious traditions and values of the old Shang and Zhou Dynasties which Confucius saw missing in the chaos of his era. This is why some of the basic ideas revolved around altruism, filial piety and respecting ancestors, knowledge, integrity, and rituals. Confucian teachings state that humans are in essence good and capable of perfection, focusing on self-improvement as well as collective improvement. In essence, it was a guide on how society should work to remain in balance, as it was seen as a micro-universe, echoing the ideas of yin and yang from the folk religion. But despite having some religious aspects, like ideas of heaven or worshiping gods, it was more focused on humanistic and familial values than on the supernatural. This is why it is sometimes seen as philosophy and sometimes as a religion, especially because it left a remarkable influence on Chinese society. But maybe it would be more precise to classify it as a way of life.

30. Han period fresco of Lao Tzu and Confucius.
Source: https://commons.wikimedia.org

In the same era, Taoism (or Daoism) was formulated. Its creator was semi-legendary thinker Lao Tzu (Laozi), who is traditionally considered to be roughly Confucius' contemporary. It was a more internal and religious philosophy, and as such, in later periods of Chinese history it did become a religion. Contrary to Confucianism, it was focused more on spiritual and physical growth than on political and social order. It harbored the ideas of non-violent actions, naturalness, life energy, nonaction, and relativism. It was rooted more in the metaphysical view of the universe and humans, and it preached personal growth through meditation and similar spiritual practices. Thus, it often looked more relaxed and kinder compared to strict Confucianism. But it also built upon the ideas of the folk religion and left a tremendous mark on Chinese society. And later Chinese forged a saying, "Practice Confucianism on the outside, Taoism on the inside" in an attempt to reconcile these two important worldviews.

In total opposition to these two was Legalism, another school of philosophical thought that emerged during the Warring States Period. This philosophical ideology didn't have any real founder but was a combination of ideas and thoughts of several government officials whose only concern was politics and power and who didn't care much about balance, morality, or the wellbeing of an individual. The focus of this philosophy was a regulated state, with a monarch on top that had the ultimate authority, with emphasis on the accumulation of wealth and power. The basic principle of achieving this was through severe and clear laws and harsh punishments, which is why it became known as Legalism. And where other schools of thought focused on universal harmony, Legalists were concerned with earthly order, safety, and stability. Thus, this ancient Chinese philosophy is often compared with realpolitik thought of Europeans. Besides the principle of law, Legalists also preached methods and arts of statesmanship as well as legitimacy and charisma. Another important ideal was a smaller central government, under stricter guidance of the emperor. And probably the most important ideal was the meritocratic filling of positions in the state bureaucracy. But as this philosophy heavily emphasized the power of the sovereign, it led to a more dictatorial rule, and it was far less popular after the fall of the Qin Dynasty. But it was influential in the development of the Chinese governmental system. Overlapping partially with Legalism was Mohism, founded by Mozi (470–391 BCE). It also dealt with politics and statesmanship but was seen more through impartial compassion. The only ideal these two philosophies agreed upon was the meritocratic system of government.

The core idea of this school of thought was unbiased consideration, as one should care about every person equally, regardless of their actual personal connection to the person in question. For Mohists, this was the true measure of a righteous man. Additionally, they saw society as an organized system in which inefficiency and wastefulness should be reduced, and thus promoted the idea that the moral worth of any action was measured to the extent of how much it contributed to society and the state. Another important idea was their opposition to fatalism and the role of destiny in life. Mohism thought this way of thinking brought poverty and sorrow as people refused to admit their own shortcomings and mistakes. But unlike other philosophical schools, Mohists also dealt with mathematics and engineering, mostly focused on siege and defense. And one of their sub-branches were the Logicians, who dealt with purely logical puzzles, paradoxes, and intellectual conundrums. This made Mohism important for scientific advancements and technological innovations for which the Chinese were famous, creating a precursor to the philosophy of scientific thought.

But all of these ideas and intellectual advances achieved through philosophy fade in comparison to the development of a writing system. This allowed for better communication and the sharing of thoughts, preserving them from being lost to time. The exact origins of the Chinese writing system are still unknown. The earliest verified examples come from 13th century BCE oracle bones of the Shang Dynasty, but their complexity at the time suggest writing was developed before then. However, some Neolithic archeological finds have some characters on them, and the earliest one is dated to around 6500 BCE. Though these characters and markings clearly aren't writing, some scholars did make some connections with the formation of the writing being developed in the Yellow River Basin. From the Shang period onward, it becomes far easier to follow the development of the Chinese writing system. By that stage, it had already passed the stage of a simple pictographic script, where each ideogram conveys its meaning through its pictorial resemblance to a physical object, and started to evolve into a logographic script in which an ideogram represents a word or a phrase. The next stage of writings was bronze and seal scripts, named after the most common objects and materials the writing was found on. These were dated from the Spring and Autumn Period as well as the Warring States Period. It further evolved into a logographic script with more complexity. It is worth noticing that during this period there were multiple local variations of the Chinese script. Previously, scholars thought that the next stage of script evolution, known as clerical script, developed from the seal script, but recent findings connect it with so-called vulgar, or common, writing.

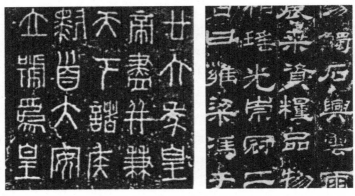

31. Examples of the seal script (left) and clerical script (right).
Source: https://commons.wikimedia.org

Proto-clerical script started to emerge in the late Warring States Period in the Qin state, as it needed a simplified and faster writing system for documents and other bureaucratic needs. With the forming of a unified China, the Qin ruler standardized the writing system based upon the clerical script. This script fully matured by the early Han, and it remained the formal script of the state administration, hence the name. This is the oldest form of the Chinese script that is still partially readable today. During the Han Dynasty, the cursive style, for quicker writing, of the clerical script was formed, and it became known as the grass script. By the late Han period, a regular script, the basis for the modern-day Chinese writing system, was formed. Many other East Asian scripts evolved from that script as well, for example, Japanese, Korean, and old Vietnamese scripts. An interesting fact about the Chinese script is that, despite not being the first in history, it is the oldest script still in use today, with an unbroken line of evolution going back at least 3,500 years. But the true importance of the development of writing cannot be stressed enough. It allowed for complex ideas and thoughts to be shared, made communication easier, and helped to spread the influence of the Chinese culture to the surrounding nations and people.

Yet literacy wasn't widespread; as this writing system was rather complicated to master, it was mostly limited to the higher scholarly classes. However, members of the elite didn't use it merely for utilitarian purposes of administration and trade. They created literary works of art, composing poems and writing down stories. With most early Chinese books of poetry, it would seem that they were just folk songs, but soon original authors, like Qu Yuan (c.340–278 BCE), appeared. Poems were often allegoric and, in some way, connected with politics and morality, though in some cases they could simply describe nature or landscapes. Of course, many philosophical works were also written down, as well as histories and annals. Probably the most influential in that respect was Sima Qian (c.145-86 BCE), whose works set up the professional historiography in China and is also the prime source for most of ancient Chinese history.

Songs and poems were also connected to music, as many of them were intended to be performed accompanied by some musical instrument. Unfortunately, these tunes have been lost to time. It is known, through paintings and archeological findings, that the ancient Chinese had a variety of instruments like guqin, a string instrument of a zither type, paixiao, a bamboo pan flute, and dizi, a common bamboo flute, as well as bronze bells and drums. In the days of the Shang Dynasty, music had a ritualistic religious purpose, but in later periods, it became more focused on entertainment. However, ceremonial court music always remained important throughout Chinese history. It's also worth noting that music was often accompanied by dances, which can be divided into two major groups. One was civilian, in which dancers carried feathers and banners while dancing, and the other was a military dance with waving weapons. These also held both entertainment and ritualistic purposes.

32. Han period fresco depicting a musician and a dancer.
Source: https://commons.wikimedia.org

Religion is also evident in ancient Chinese sculptures, as the early bronze vessels were cast primarily to be used in rituals. They had intricate zoomorphic decorations and complicated patterns but avoided human form, which became predominant in later periods. Jade sculptures and carvings also played an important role as it was one of the most popular and highly sought-after materials in China, as it was connected with health and immortality, and often used for burial objects. Even today, jade is commonly associated with Chinese culture. Of course, as time passed, the skill of the Chinese artisans grew, as did the quality of their figurines and sculptures. In later periods, clay was also used for sculpting, and the best example of this is the Terracotta Army found in the first emperor's tomb.

33. Archeological site of the Terracotta Army.
Source: https://commons.wikimedia.org

It was a collection of about 8,000 life-sized sculptures of warriors of all ranks that were supposed to accompany the deceased emperor in his afterlife. They were all sculpted with their armor on, and the features depended on their rank and unit type. All of them were armed with real bronze weapons, but most of them were looted before archeologists found the tomb. This, combined with the fact that there were also sculptures of horses and chariots, brought a high level of realism in representing the ancient Chinese army, with the final layer being bright colors that once adorned the soldiers. Unfortunately, that final finishing touch has degraded over time, leaving us today with sculptures of terracotta color. This magnificent work of art has captivated the imagination of many generations, showcasing just how capable the artists and artisans of early imperial China were. Another type of pottery, for which the Chinese are much more famous, is porcelain. It first started emerging during the Autumn and Spring Period, but true porcelain, as we know it today, was created only during the Han Dynasty. The finest pieces of porcelain were of course reserved for the emperor and the elite, complete with lavish decorations and vivid colors. At the time, they were often used as diplomatic gifts and for burial purposes, as well as for everyday use.

Paintings, on the other hand, were only used as decorations. The first decorative paintings on pottery vessels were merely patterns and shapes, but from the Warring States Period onward, the focus of artists shifted to the world around them. One example of that was frescos, painted in the tombs and temples, depicting humans in various activities. They were often scenes of triumphs or great achievements of the ruler, generals, or other prominent men. Other less permanent objects were used for painting as well, like silk or wooden folding screens. In some cases, ceramics were also painted on. And it is during the Han Dynasty that the first examples of landscapes in Chinese art were found. These types of paintings were often done by nobles, who had enough time to practice the fine brushwork needed to create these paintings. Artistic calligraphy is also connected with those. Its traces can be found during the Han period when the cursive script was formed. This skill was often highly appreciated, as it required elegance and patience, and together with painting, it was seen as the purest forms of art. Thanks to paintings, we can see other details about Chinese lifestyle, like the brightly colored silk tunics today known as hanfu. Of course, silk and high-quality furs were reserved for the nobles. Commoners usually wore clothes made out of hemp or wool.

Another major difference between commoners and the elite was the houses they lived in. Commoners' houses were often made out of mud and wood with a thatched roof. They were commonly rectangular with small inner courtyards. The village homes were sometimes connected with barns for farm animals, which were often adjacent to the main house. Floors were sometimes covered with clay or straw, and in other cases, they usually were simple dirt floors. On the other hand, nobles lived in lavish palaces and villas, commonly made out of clay bricks and stone, which were much more durable and better insulated, with decorated wooden roofs and beams. They were also rather colorful, with yellow being reserved for imperial palaces. Palaces were usually complexes of several buildings and also had inner courtyards. Contrary to most Western cultures, the Chinese put a lesser emphasis on the height of their buildings, focusing more on width to impress. This is why vaults and arches, which weren't needed as much, are not a prominent feature of their architecture, even though they existed in tombs and on city gates. Another important feature of ancient Chinese architecture was its use of expression and bilateral symmetry, signifying balance and order that is so vital to their culture. This was also seen in the grand gardens built by the elites, creating enclosed parks with forests and ponds, and adorned with flower and pavilions. First built during the Shang Dynasty, these ancient Chinese gardens attempted to express the harmony that should exist between nature and humans by crafting idealized miniature landscapes. Interestingly, most of the architectural features of the ancient Chinese civilization survived with little innovations until modern times.

34. Modern model of an ancient Chinese city.
Source: https://commons.wikimedia.org

Looking at the culture of the ancient Chinese people, two things become clear. Firstly, it evolved from a religious background, focusing more on the supernatural and deistic, developing into a civilization concerned more about humans and earthly life. Though religion and ancestral veneration never subsided, it became much less concerned with gods than Western civilizations. And secondly, it is clear that the basis of Chinese civilization founded by the end of the Han Dynasty to this day remains set in that foundation. This makes Chinese culture rather consistent, rooted in the ancient past and traditions set over 2,000 years ago. This proves the longevity and strength of the Chinese civilization, and it is why it is one of the most important in the world today.

Chapter 8 – Inventions and Innovations of the Ancient Chinese

During the period of ancient Chinese history covered in this guide, the Chinese civilization went through some significant changes, actually becoming what we associate with China today. These changes gifted the world with some of the most remarkable inventions and innovations, some being so important that they changed the world, while others show an interesting insight in how thinkers of past ages thought and solved problems. Because of this, in this chapter we'll go over some of the advancements achieved by the Chinese during this time, illuminating another part of their civilization and showing one more aspect of why it became so influential and important for world history.

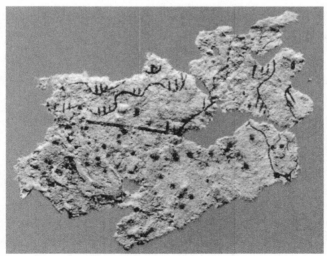

35. Oldest found paper fragment from 179 BCE.
Source: https://commons.wikimedia.org

It would be only appropriate to start with probably the most important and influential invention that the ancient Chinese gave to the world—paper. Today it might not seem like such an important innovation, but it actually transformed the world by making it easier to spread the written word, thus speeding up the spread of ideas and knowledge. Before, paper rolls of bamboo strips or silk were used for writing in China. Bamboo was bulky and awkward to carry around and store, while silk was simply too expensive for common use. In the rest of the world, they used papyrus, clay tablets, or parchment for writing, but they all had similar drawbacks. But during the Han Dynasty, according to myth, a court official looking at wasps building their nest became inspired to create paper from the bark of trees, rags of cloth, fishing nets, and remnants of hemp. And according to this story, this invention happened around 105 CE. But archeological findings go as far as the 2nd century BCE, but the first use for writing on paper is evidenced in 8 BCE. It was light and cheap material, easy for everyday use. Originally, it seems it was used for wrapping and padding of bronze mirrors. Unfortunately, the Han Dynasty didn't survive long enough to see the true explosion of paper used as a writing material, but this was still a crucial step in revolutionizing communication.

From previous chapters, it is clear that casting metal was something that the Chinese mastered early on. The earliest known cast iron was indeed found in China as far back as the 5th century BCE. But by the Han Dynasty, the Chinese refined their metal casting technology and techniques. Beforehand, they were using blast furnaces to melt iron ore in unpurified pig iron. Then they used cupola furnaces to remelt the pig iron into purified cast iron. To put this advance in perspective, modern cupola furnaces were invented in 18th century France. By 300 BCE, they discovered that through the process of decarburization, or by introducing excess amounts of air in cupola furnaces, they could produce higher quality wrought iron. It was actually wrought iron that was used for weapons and tools, making bronze finally obsolete. During the 2nd century BCE, they also realized that by combining cast and wrought iron they could create steel, a more useful and durable metal alloy. For that, they used finery forges and the so-called puddling process of stirring the molten metal with rods, both more than a thousand years before Europeans, even though steel was known since the Roman times. Their ingenuity went further as they harnessed waterpower through water-powered reciprocators to run the bellows on furnaces, reducing the need for hard manual labor in the metalmaking process.

Of course, two other inventions were needed for that technology to be implemented. The First, and arguably more important, one was the waterwheel. They weren't the first ones to invent it, as that title most likely goes to the ancient Egyptians, but the Chinese did develop it on their own, as the early waterwheel of the Han Dynasty was horizontal. Besides being used as a part of a water-powered reciprocator in the metal industry, they found their use in agriculture as well. From their use of pestle and mortar, the ancient Chinese developed water-powered trip hammers they used for thrashing, decorticating, and polishing grain. Hydraulic power was also harvested by chain pumps connected to the waterwheel, which were used to lift the water into irrigation channels. This system was also adapted to lift the water into a stoneware pipe system of the imperial palace and nobles' living quarters, creating, in essence, an ancient plumbing system. But the waterwheel wasn't the only invention needed to make a water-powered reciprocator. They also needed a belt drive, which was created during the 1st century BCE. This was a system in which belts were used to link two rotating shafts to transmit power. The first recorded use of a belt drive was in quilling devices that were used to wind silk fibers onto spools. In the reciprocator mechanism, it was used to connect the waterwheel shafts with the bellows.

Mechanical ingenuity of the ancient Chinese didn't stop there. The earliest crank handles, which were operated by hand, were discovered in China dating to the 2nd century BCE. They were used to power fans in a winnowing machine used to separate the chaff from the grain. In later periods, this technology was adapted for other uses. Ancient Chinese engineers also developed the gear as early as the 4th century BCE. They were both made out of wood, but also from cast bronze and metal. Their applications were numerous, as it transmitted harnessed waterpower to finer mechanical creations like the odometer cart, which measured covered distances thanks to a complex system of gears powered by the rotation of the wheels. Chinese inventiveness and understanding of nature can also be seen through their invention of the first seismograph that showed the direction of earthquakes. It did so thanks to a pendulum inside a bronze vessel that would swing as the earth shook, hitting a mechanism on one of the eight sides that represented major directions of the earth. The crank-and-catch mechanism would then release a metal ball that would drop and alert people nearby with its loud noise that an earthquake would happen. Their observance of nature can also be seen in their early lodestone compasses. Lodestone is simply naturally magnetized mineral, which when freely suspended point to the magnetic poles of the Earth. But these weren't used for navigation for another ten centuries; instead, they were utilized for geomancy and fortune telling.

36. Han Dynasty era mold for a bronze gear.
Source: https://commons.wikimedia.org

The Ancient Chinese also made several advances in medicine, despite it being firmly rooted in religious and philosophical practices, as it was connected with the ideas of life force, balance, and harmony. Chinese physicians realized that the ephedra plant, which contains ephedrine, could be used as an antiasthmatic and stimulant. They practiced dietary treatments and prescribed preventive exercises, similar to present-day Tai Chi, and it is during these ancient times that the practice of acupuncture was developed. Their physicians were keen observers, so they were able to recognize and describe symptoms of leprosy and diabetes, though they didn't have a proper cure for these illnesses.

But the physicians weren't the only ones in the Chinese society proficient in observing and noting natural occurrences. By the end of the 2nd century CE, Chinese astronomers had cataloged over 2,500 stars and 120 constellations. To represent them and to aid astronomers with the calendrical computations and calculations, they had built an armillary sphere (spherical astrolabe) during the 1st century BCE, roughly at the same time as Westerners did. But later Chinese armillary spheres were made automatized by hydraulic power. And it was the Chinese astronomers who observed the first sunspot in the mid-4th century BCE. By the time of the Han Dynasty, they theorized that light came only from the sun and that moon and planets were only reflecting that light. And like many other ancient civilizations, they knew about only five planets, Mars, Jupiter, Venus, Saturn, and Mercury, all of which are visible to the naked eye. They also believed that the sun, moon, and planets were actually spherical balls, despite still supporting the idea of a geocentric universe.

Lowering their gaze from the stars, the ancient Chinese focused on the earth beneath them. The earliest map dates from the 4th century BCE, showing the tributary river systems of the Jialing River in present-day Sichuan, along with administrative counties, roads, as well as timber gathering sites and their distances to them, being possibly the oldest economic map found so far. They also wrote books with geographical information, describing the traditional nine provinces, their characteristic goods, type of soil and agriculture systems, and even their revenues. The oldest such book dates to the 5th century BCE. During the Han Dynasty rule, cartography was further developed, and Chinese maps became more detailed and precise. Cartographers also started creating relief maps. An interesting change was made in their evolution as Qin maps placed north at the top, while Han cartographers put south on top.

Going further down into the earth below, the Chinese also pioneered new types of mining techniques called borehole drilling. The drill would be rotated by draft animals while several men jumped on top of it to create a narrow shaft that reportedly could reach depths of up to 600 m (2,000 ft). They were most often used to mine for brine, a high-concentration solution of salt in water. To extract the salt, they boiled the brine. According to some archeological findings, while they were mining for brine, they stumbled upon natural gas. By 500 BCE, they found a way to use it, transporting it from the ground in crude pipelines of bamboo, by boiling the salty water. Besides being the first to utilize natural gas by the 1st century BCE, they had also found and started to use unrefined crude oil.

But observation and practical use weren't the only scientific fields in which the ancient Chinese excelled. They also achieved several impressive mathematical breakthroughs. In the Shang era, they had already developed basic arithmetic, a decimal system, and equations. Historians aren't sure if they also adopted the idea of negative numbers at that time, but by the Han Dynasty, they surely did. So, while most of the Hellenistic and Roman world saw negative numbers as an invalid result, the Chinese saw it as a viable solution, as it represented a duality represented in their idea of yin and yang. By the end of the Han Dynasty, Chinese mathematicians had also calculated pi to 3.14 and created their own Pythagoras' Theorem known as Gougu Theorem, meaning they also understood the ideas of a square cube and square root. Besides being the first civilization to adopt the idea of negative numbers, they also left the earliest evidence of a decimal fraction in the 1st century CE. The most developed achievement of ancient Chinese mathematics was creating the Gaussian elimination (row reduction), an algorithm used to solve linear equations by the end of the 2nd century CE. This was achieved in Europe only in the early 18th century. From the mathematical textbooks written down during the Han rule, it is clear that their math first developed as a need for trade, then improved for the needs of the state, calculating taxes and surfaces of plots, as well as dividing labor and other administrative tasks. Only by the late Han, when mathematics got advanced enough, did it become more focused on solely resolving theoretical problems.

37. Model of the Warring States Period traction trebuchet.
Source: https://commons.wikimedia.org

Less theoretical and more practical were the Chinese advances and inventions in military equipment. The most notable invention was, of course, the crossbow. The oldest archeological evidence of it is dated to the mid-7th century BCE. Crossbows remained the most valued weapon among the ancient Chinese. In later periods of the Warring States Period, crossbows were enlarged and mounted on wall towers, and used for both attack and defense. And the design of the crossbow itself became more sophisticated over time, with more precise and stronger mechanisms, as well as becoming lighter and easier to use. From the 5th century BCE, Chinese were also using war wagons on the battlefield, which served as a mobile armored cart to protect the soldiers. Most often it was used during sieges, to protect the archers or the tunnel diggers from the defender's projectiles. By the 4th century BCE, traction trebuchet, also known as mangonel, was created, which used manpower to hurl large pieces of stone at defenses of a city with high accuracy and rate of fire. During the Spring and Autumn Period, the first accounts of martial arts appear in military textbooks. This is a hand-to-hand combat system that includes techniques such as strikes, joint manipulation, pressure point attacks, and throws. From these early beginnings, the famous

Chinese martial arts developed, becoming one of the recognizable signatures of their civilization.

Some other innovation made by the ancient Chinese could be described more as cultural than anything else, but nonetheless tied in with their civilization and influence with other cultures. Probably the most iconic and influential are chopsticks. The earliest found date to around 1200 BCE, and they were made out of bronze. But scholars think they were invented long before that, at least during the mythical Xia Dynasty, if not further back to the Neolithic times. Their use has spread across East Asia and now are irreversibly connected with our notion of Asian cuisine. Another invention connected with Chinese cooking are woks and stir-frying. There are indications of them being used in the Spring and Autumn Period, but the oldest confirmed wok dates from the Han Dynasty. It should be noted that boiling and steaming remained more popular in traditional Chinese cuisine until the late Middle Ages. Another Chinese innovation that has spread across the world is drinking tea. Chinese have been drinking tea, going as far back as the Shang Dynasty, at first as a medicinal and ritualistic drink, but later as a stimulative drink. Another food-related novelty devised by the ancient Chinese is soy paste and sauce. Created by the Chinese during the Han Dynasty, they were used as a way to stretch out the use of salt, which was rather expensive. Ancient Chinese enjoyed sports as well, one of them being cuju, a Chinese variation of football (soccer), that involved kicking a ball through a hole in a net. It was first used as a military exercise in the 3rd century BCE, but during the Han Dynasty, it became the sport of the nobles. Despite dying out later on, today it's recognized by FIFA as the earliest form of football in history.

There are many more inventions, innovations, and knowledge with which the ancient Chinese have influenced the world and its development. This just goes to show how advanced their civilization had become by the start of the imperial era, having numerous inventive men looking for ways to improve the lives of other people around them. So, it goes to show that the old Western notion of Europe being a center of technological and scientific superiority is a simple misconception created in the European colonial era. The Warring States Period, alongside with the Han Dynasty rule, was the first burst of scholarly and technological leaps made by the Chinese people, leaving inventions that are often seen as modern technology. And it once again shows why the Chinese civilization is so important and why it should be studied.

Conclusion

Looking at the history of ancient China, several things become evident. It is a civilization that was created and made its first steps in isolation, far away from other cultures. This is why many of its ideas and foundations seem so different from most others of the time. Yet, looking at how it developed, it becomes clear that no matter how different it may seem it had gone through ups and downs like any other civilization, showing that beneath the layers of culture and history lays something that connects us all—humanity. Despite how far apart civilizations grow and how unique they are, the human spirit is what moves it. And that is why Chinese history is also filled with numerous great men, generals, inventors, and philosophers, as well as conspirators, tyrants, and decadent drunks. In that aspect, ancient Chinese civilization is no exception.

But at the same time, thanks to the very unique path it took in its development, Chinese civilization and society remain strikingly different from Western cultures. And this difference is visible even today, as the root of modern Chinese culture lies in foundations set in ancient times. But different shouldn't mean worse or bad. Just by reading this short introductory guide, it should be clear that ancient China achieved many feats. On a political scale, it managed to conquer vast areas and unite tens of millions of people under one border and government. From humble beginnings, China indeed became a strong and wealthy empire. And Chinese people managed to create stunning pieces of art, gather tremendous knowledge, and build many wondrous inventions. Its ideals were equality and welfare for all, striving for balance and harmony. Looking at all this, it becomes clear how and why ancient China is so influential. But one thing should be emphasized: these were only the first steps of Chinese civilization. It was still in its youth. In those first 2,000 years, it went through many changes and upheavals, but it prevailed. Since then, almost 2,000 more years have passed, and this culture is still going strong, slowly rising back to the top as the strongest, wealthiest, and most technologically advanced country in the world. And looking at its past, it is in its rightful place.

At the same time, learning about ancient Chinese history reminds us that human civilization didn't develop from only one center and didn't follow one simple straight line. Too often, the Western world disregards other cultures and civilizations, thinking their histories are less significant. But it is important to remember that humanity is diverse: it grew from many roots, each civilization giving something to mankind, which influenced the development of the global world civilization that we have today. One of these roots is ancient China.

In the end, hopefully this guide has piqued your interest to find out more about ancient China and Chinese civilization in general. Because knowing and appreciating our collective past is important if we want to understand each other and comprehend the present, and if we want to develop a better future together.

Short Timeline of Ancient Chinese History

c. 2070 BCE - Mythical Xia Dynasty was created

c. 1600 BCE - Rise of the Shang Dynasty

c. 1350 BCE - Anyang becomes Shang capital, start of the Shang golden age

c. 1250 BCE - Oldest remains of Chinese script found on oracle bones

1250 to 1192 BCE - Reign of greatest Shang king Wu Ding

1046 BCE - A grand battle of Muye and the start of Zhou Dynasty

957 BCE - Zhou expansion stopped by death of King Zhao

841 BCE - Revolt against the Zhou rule and exile of the King Li

771 BCE - The Zhou court moves east and the start of the Autumn and Spring Period

7th century BCE - Invention of the crossbow

667 BCE - Duke Huan of Qi becomes first hegemon

551 to 479 BCE - Life and works of Confucius

546 BCE - Jin, Chu, Qi, and Qin states arrange truce and divide spheres of influence

5th century BCE - Invention of cast iron technology

476 BCE - Beginning of the Warring States Period

470 to 391 BCE - Life and work of Mozi

458 to 403 BCE - Partition of Jin

344 BCE - Rulers of Qi and Wei become first kings outside the ruling dynasty

288 BCE - Rulers of Qi and Qin attempt to proclaim themselves emperors

269 BCE - Defeat of Qin and start of the king Zhao's reforms

247 BCE - Zhao Zheng became king of Qin

230 to 221 BCE - Final unification of China, King Zhao becomes Qin Shi Huangdi

210 BCE - Death of Qin Shi Huangdi

206 BCE - Fall of Qin Dynasty

202 BCE - Liu Bang becomes Emperor Gaozu and starts the Han Dynasty

2nd century BCE - Invention of paper

180 to 157 BCE - Reforms and rule of Emperor Wen

145 to 86 BCE - Life and work Sima Qian, establishing Chinese historiography

141 to 87 BCE - Conquests and expansion of China under rule of Emperor Wu

9 CE - Wang Mang's coup and attempt to establish a new dynasty

22 CE - Peasant uprising in former state of Qin

25 CE - Restoration of the Han Dynasty and moving of the capital to the east

57 to 88 CE - Rules of emperors Ming and Zhang, golden age of the Han Dynasty

125 to 144 CE - Development of education and science under Emperor Shun

161 CE - Emperor Huan starts selling administrative offices, weakening and corrupting the government

184 CE - The Yellow Turban Rebellion begins, led by a Taoist preacher

189 to 220 CE - Reign of the Emperor Xian and the fall of Han Dynasty

Part 2: Ancient Japan

A Captivating Guide to the Ancient History of Japan, Their Ancient Civilization, and Japanese Culture, Including Stories of the Samurai, Shōguns, and Zen Masters

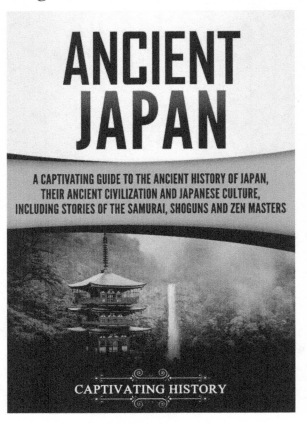

Introduction

Japan, the country of the rising sun, is today known as one of the most prosperous and technologically advanced nations despite not having many natural resources. It is full of hardworking, ethical people that live with a mix of old-time traditions and new-age progressive lifestyles. It's the land of famed and virtuous samurai warriors, for whom loyalty is everything, and of legendary and adept ninja assassins, capable of bypassing any obstacle. No less famed is Japanese art, unique in its style and form, from short haiku songs to breathtaking watercolor paintings, both amazingly vivid and simplistic in form. It's the country of Buddhist Zen masters, who were wise and spiritual, symbols of moderation and morality. At the same time, it's the culture of geishas, who represented indulgence, entertainment, and corporeal desires. Today, it is one of the most liberal and democratic countries, yet it still has an emperor on the throne and a long tradition of shōguns, who were more or less military dictators. All in all, Japan seems to be a country of paradoxes and oppositions, of yin and yang.

Yet it doesn't seem to suffer from it; instead, it is thriving, growing, and developing, and it has been doing so for a long time. From those contradictions, a sense of unity and pride arose, guiding Japanese history and civilizational development through the ages, leaving an unquestionable mark on the world heritage and mankind. But this is only the surface of an astonishing culture that deserves a deeper look. This guide will lead you into that dive, showing how those characteristics synonymous with the Japanese civilization gradually appeared, formed, and transformed through time. Learning about Japan's history, its past failures and successes and how they shaped their nation, will also illuminate how this civilization developed, while at the same time presenting a full array of interesting stories, persons, and events. Hopefully, this guide will leave you wanting to learn more about Japan, to understand its people and culture better, as it is only a first step in the thousand-mile journey that is Japanese history.

Chapter 1 – Origins of Imperial Japan and Its People

In the beginning, there was chaos. Japanese mythology, like so many throughout human history, begins with this sentence. Over time that chaos divided into pure heaven and unwholesome earth, or rather, the never-ending ocean. As these two grew apart, seven pairs of gods and goddesses emerged from the reed that started to arise from the watery surface below the sky. Among them most important were Izanagi and Izanami, god and goddess of creation. From the floating bridge of heaven, they stabbed the never-ending ocean with a jewel-decorated spear. A drop of water that fell from the spear tip into the ocean coagulated into the first island, the first solid soil on earth. The two of them moved to the newly-created land and later decided to get married. From that union, Izanami gave birth to other islands, seas, rivers, plants, and trees. During that time, other gods were created as well. Izanagi himself gave life to Amaterasu, the sun goddess, and Tsukuyomi, the moon god. With the two of them, day and night were created. This is how the ancient Japanese imagined the creation of the Japanese archipelago, a series of about seven thousand islands that spreads from the Sea of Okhotsk northeast to the Philippine Sea south along the northeastern coast of the Asian continent.

Painting of Izanami (left) and Izanagi (right).
Source: https://commons.wikimedia.org

Of course, most of these islands are small and almost insignificant, but four of them stand out as the major Japanese isles. Going from north to south those islands are Hokkaido, Honshu, Shikoku, and Kyushu. And despite looking rather small on the world maps, Japan has an area of about 378,000 km² (146,000 mi²). To put in perspective, it is roughly the size of Germany or the US state of Montana. It is a considerable land mass that is separated from Korea and the rest of Asia by the Tsushima Strait which is at least 65 km (40 mi) wide at its narrowest. That means the influence from the Asian mainland was limited, although not nonexistent as it was previously thought. The fact that about half of the land of Japan is mountainous adds to its inaccessibility but also reflects the volcanic origins of the archipelago. Even the most famous natural landmark of Japan, Mt. Fuji, is a dormant volcano. And as the Japanese archipelago is situated on the edge of the Pacific volcanic ring, where the earth's tectonic plates collide, it presently has more than 100 active volcanoes and often suffers from terrible natural disasters like earthquakes, tsunamis, and, of course, volcanic eruptions.

Topographical map of Japan. Source: https://commons.wikimedia.org

At first, it may seem that these islands aren't that hospitable because of this. Yet the volcanic ash created arable land, which constitutes about 11.5% of Japan's total area, making it rather fertile and capable of supporting a large population. The rest of the land is covered by forests, cities, roads, mountains, and lakes. Of course, the actual percentage of the land used for agriculture was way smaller in the past as it grew with the rise of population, which numbers today around 126 million. To put matters further in perspective, the entire population lives on about 5% of the land because of the landscape, explaining why most people feel this country is rather small. Another important characteristic of the Japanese archipelago is its diverse climate. On Hokkaido, in the north, winters are cold and summers are relatively mild. Honshu has a slightly warmer climate, characterized by a more distinctive difference in temperature between winter and summer. The Pacific coast of this Japanese island also has a somewhat warmer and rainier climate than the coast looking toward the Asian continent. Going farther south to Kyushu, the weather gets rather warm and humid with heavy rainfall, becoming distinctively subtropical.

Seeing how attractive the climate, safe, isolated areas, and fertile lands could seem to the early settlers, it would be easy to assume these were the reasons for the first migrations from the Asian mainland to the Japanese isles. But that's not the case. The first humans to settle there came somewhere between 500,000 and 30,000 years ago, though the general scientific agreement dates the first settlers to Japan around 200,000 years before our time. At that time, humans were still hunter-gatherers, so the most likely reason why they moved from mainland Asia to the Japanese archipelago was that they were following their prey, large game like deer and bison. And they were able to move there because during the last ice age there were land bridges, as sea levels were lower than today, that connected Japan with the Asian mainland both to the north, to what is today eastern Russia, and to the south, present-day China. This allowed small groups of early humans to move to these lands, with the highest estimates of the total population never exceeding 20,000 in that period. But around 15,000 years ago, the ice started to melt, as the ice age was coming to an end, and the land bridges were lost, isolating to a certain degree the remaining population on the islands.

At the same time, with a warmer climate the land became more fertile, and hunter-gatherer groups, that most likely never exceeded 150 people, started to shift to a more sedentary way of life, creating more specialized settlements that allowed for early primitive trade. Archeologists found evidence of obsidian, a volcanic glass used for toolmaking, being traded in an area that spanned over 150 km (93 mi). The trading zone of this material also crossed over the sea, indicating that watercraft were being used by a rather early era. And the earliest signs of pottery in Japan are dated to around 13,000 BCE, making them one of the oldest in the world, if not the oldest ever found. This is used to mark the transition from a Paleolithic to a Neolithic age in Japan and marks the beginning of the Jōmon period in Japanese history. It was named after a cord pattern, called jōmon in Japanese, which most of the pottery was decorated with. The first signs of a sedentary lifestyle have been found during this period, with the most important being the earliest indications of agriculture from around 4000 BCE, larger tribal villages with populations going up to about 500, and the pottery itself. But most of the groups remained hunter-gatherers with only semi-permanent camp-like settlements.

These groups were still largely focused on hunting and probably even more prominently on fishing, as it seems that the majority of Jōmon settlements were found on the coast. During this period, their societies achieved several important advances. For example, in technological terms, they developed the production of hemp clothing around 5000 BCE and lacquerware in 4000 BCE. In social terms, there are signs of spiritual development in the form of shamanism seen through ritual figurines, burial sites, and enigmatic stone circles. As uniquely specialized members of the community, shamans, along with tribal chiefs and perhaps the more capable hunters and farmers, were slowly starting to form an elite class, though it is still a matter of debate among scholars if the Jōmon society was more egalitarian or hierarchical in nature. However, it was by no means a completely isolated or homogenized society. It had various local subcultures and regional characteristics, while rice and millet were introduced from the Asian mainland, most likely China, around 1000 BCE, clearly showing that foreign influence existed. Before that, people most commonly cultivated the beefsteak herb and barnyard grass. The arrival of rice also marks the beginning of the end of the Jōmon period, according to some historians.

As the rice was brought by the newcomers from the mainland, the spread of its domestication is seen as evidence of the first wave of foreign invasion. It culminated around 400 BCE, leading most scholars to see this period of time as the definitive end of the Jōmon era and culture. The foreigners, known as the Yayoi, pushed the Jōmon people north. The Yayoi had narrower faces and were slightly taller compared to the Jōmon, whose males were on average 157 cm (5.15 ft) tall and whose females were only 148 cm (4.85 ft), both with a stocky constitution and wide, square faces. The Yayoi were also more technologically advanced as they had knowledge of metallurgy and were more focused on agriculture. For a long time, it was thought that the Jōmon people simply perished over time under the pressure of their conquerors, but recent studies by physical anthropologists confirm that their direct descendants are the Ainu minority that today live on Hokkaido. For centuries, the Ainu people suffered a great deal of oppression and marginalization by the Japanese people, who bear a much higher resemblance to the Yayoi invaders. Today, the Ainu are treated a bit better as in 2008 the Japanese government officially recognized them as the indigenous Japanese population. But the motivation and origins of the Yayoi people, as well as the actual scale and character of their migration or invasion, remains a matter of debate among modern historians.

What is certain is that by 400 BCE the Yayoi period began, which is named after a district in Tokyo where in the late 19th century a new type of reddish pottery was found, indicating a break from former Jōmon traditions. And it was a major break, as the newcomers lived in a completely sedentary agricultural lifestyle, based around rice cultivation. They brought with themselves the technology of paddies, making its farming more efficient. Thanks to that, rice became a staple food for the Japanese, practically one of their cultural foundations, which remains to this day. And with agricultural development came the population explosion. From about 100,000 inhabitants in the late Jōmon period, Japan became home to about 1.5 to 2 million people by the end of the Yayoi era in the 3rd century CE. With that came larger settlements, with the largest covering an area of about 200 acres, which was at least 3 times larger than any settlement from the previous age. At the same time, agricultural development brought about the narrowing of resources available to the entire community, and the first true elites started to appear around the families that had control over rice production.

A jar from the Yayoi period. Source: https://commons.wikimedia.org

This was further emphasized by the rise of trade between the tribes. Some were settled in the regions that had metal ores, which are rather scarce in Japan, while others had agricultural surpluses or produced silk (technology which was also imported from China), pottery, glass, or metal products. But the trade remained in the hands of the wealthiest, further elevating them from the commoners. With that, society changed as well. Tribes developed into more territorial chiefdoms, with warfare escalating between them in a fight to control vital territories. Warfare was the final element that solidified the position of the elites as they were the only ones capable of both wielding metal weapons and gathering large forces to wage wars. At the same time, prisoners were becoming slaves, creating the lowest social class, although it never became as influential as it was in ancient Rome or Greece. This social stratification was an important change, ending the previously more egalitarian community. And as warfare continued, chiefdoms started to ally with one another, growing through conquest and creating a large number of rather small political communities which we today identify as kingdoms. Their power also grew which became evident by the fact that by the late 1st century CE, they were capable of sending envoys to the Chinese empire, looking for an external ally in one of the strongest world powers of the time.

These connections with the already fully developed Chinese civilization leaves us with some rare detailed glimpses into Japanese history, as the Chinese historians of that era wrote about Japan as well. At first, they called it the land of Wa, meaning land of dwarfs, and they noted that it consisted of 100 small kingdoms. By the mid-3rd century, Chinese writers give us more detailed looks, describing in more detail Yamatai (Hsieh-ma-t'ai in Chinese) as the strongest of the Japanese kingdoms. They report this kingdom was ruled by Queen Himiko, a female shaman and a strong figure which was recognized by the Chinese as the ruler of the entirety of Japan, though it is unclear if her influence was that strong. She supposedly lived secluded in a fortress, served by 1,000 women and 1 man, guarded by 100 soldiers, and accessible only to her brother, who dealt with the day-to-day state affairs. Chinese reports tell us that Himiko herself was involved with magic and sorcery and that she remained unmarried. She ascended to the throne after a long period of wars in Japan around 180 CE, and she ruled until her death in 248 CE, which afterward Yamatai fell once again into turmoil. Reportedly, a king was chosen, but no one wanted to obey him, so a new queen, 13-year-old Iyo, who was Himiko's relative, was picked as a new ruler.

These details, like the exact location of Yamatai which some scholars place in northern Kyushu or central Honshu, are marked with a dose of uncertainty, as no other evidence of them have been found. No archeological sites have been unearthed, and no Japanese sources from that era exist, as later histories omit Himiko, either by lack of knowledge or because female rulers didn't fit the imperial narrative. But more important details are the Chinese depictions of customs and life in Japan, which historians usually accept as true. They note that Japanese people were fond of drinking and ate with their hands, which is corroborated by the lack of any eating utensils found in graves of the Yayoi period. The hierarchy was important, as people from the lower classes would step aside from the road and bow to the member of a higher class, showing his respect. Nobles were allowed to have several wives and usually had attendants or slaves. They practiced divination by burning bones, which was also corroborated by archeological findings, and buried their dead in a single coffin. The Yayoi Japanese made clothes out of silk, linen, cotton, and hemp, while they used bronze to make religious items, like mirrors or bells, and in some occasions weapons as well. Iron was usually reserved for weapons and in some cases agricultural tools, as it was more durable.

Modern illustration of Queen Himiko.
Source: https://commons.wikimedia.org

All of those items, along with food, chiefly rice, was used for trade, which Chinese sources say happened in centralized markets which could be found in every district. And though modern scholars aren't certain how exactly those early kingdoms functioned, Chinese writers note that their governments were indeed able to gather taxes or tributes from their subjects. This meant that by the end of the Yayoi period these early Japanese states were growing into fully functional shamanistic monarchies with distinctive social stratification. The Yayoi rulers were indeed increasing their power, and their states were increasingly centralized and territorial. Those economic, political, social, and technological changes of this period were indeed a first step toward the unification into a singular Japanese state. And they also facilitated the creation of an amalgamated Japanese civilization, as in these centuries, there were many local cultural variations. As those transformations were peaking around the time of Himiko's death, the Yayoi period was coming to an end. The power of the state at the time became evident in burial traditions. Tradition states that her tomb was a large mound, 100 m (328 ft) in diameter, where her immolated servants, both male and female, were buried as well. Indeed, in the late 3rd century CE, burial mounds became a common tradition for rulers and members of the elite, marking a beginning of a new period of Japanese history.

Those burial mounds, known as kofun in Japanese, gave the name to the new era. It was an era where the power of the state grew rapidly, seen in its ability to create large tombs filled with various items for the afterlife as well as numerous weapons. Besides proving the wealth of the deceased, those arms were also showcasing the force that the elite was able to wield to protect its position in power. This rise in power was followed by smaller kingdoms or chiefdoms being incorporated or conquered by the larger and stronger ones. So instead of a hundred smaller states, there were several larger kingdoms. The most important of these was the Yamato kingdom, located in the Nara Basin in the southwestern parts of Honshu, between the present-day cities of Osaka and Kyoto. Because of the similar name, some historians link it with the Yamatai of Queen Himiko, but so far, this theory hasn't been proven. But the kingdom of Yamato did start to rise in prominence in the late 3rd century CE. It was a slow and gradual process as Yamato kings were expanding their power and authority primarily through negotiation, persuasion, and coercion and less through simple military conquest.

Later period kofun (upper image) and copper jewelry found in another kofun (lower image). Source: https://commons.wikimedia.org

This is evident by the fact that the most common method of expansion used by Yamato kings was to incorporate already existing states and chiefdoms into their kingdom, integrating subjugated rulers into the Yamato hierarchy by giving them titles and ranks. That way, they would become part of the ruling structure and less willing to rebel as they would have personal stakes and connections with the developing imperial system. Another benefit of that approach is that the kingdom of Yamato wasn't confronting possible threats around it; rather, they assimilated powerful enemies and then used their potential in further expansion instead of simply destroying it. A byproduct of that way of thinking and organization was the highly hierarchical social and state system, in which rank was the ultimate measure of one's worth. And it became such a staple of Japanese society that in a certain way it still lives in Japan today. But a negative side of that kind of expansion was that it was slow and meticulous. So, during the 4th and 5th centuries CE, Yamato didn't achieve absolute supremacy over surrounding kingdoms. It was, at most, the first among equals. But as no written records of these times exist, we have no exact details how this expansion and growth in power exactly unfolded.

What seems certain was that the Yamato state lacked a proper unity, thanks to its absorption of the other states around it. The main loyalty of a man was to his clan or kin, called uji in Japanese. One's fidelity to the Yamato king depended solely on how loyal the clan chief was. Those were more or less the outlines of the earliest Japanese states the Chinese wrote about in the 1st and 2nd centuries. The clan members became the militaristic noble class, creating a base for the Japanese elite that lasted until the late 19th century. The hierarchy was also strong in the kin organization, as all members had to follow orders of the clan head. Besides deciding the faith of the family on this earth, clan superiors were also tasked with appeasing the gods on behalf of all their kin. Below them were occupational groups known as be, which were social groupings of people related to the profession they worked in. This is why this class was sometimes translated as "guild" in English, but that is rather incorrect. A similarity exists as they provided specialized functions in a society, such as metalsmiths, weavers, priests, or palace guards, or even provided household duties in the elite's courts. But those were only a minority of be groups; most were in fact farmers. And unlike guilds, they had a similar hierarchical structure as clans, with a singular head of the family being in charge. And one's affiliation with a certain be was hereditary. Also, there was a fictional connection between the uji and be, with the latter being organized to serve and aid the uji. All of this combined makes be groups rather different than European guilds.

The expansion of Yamato in that period wasn't linked only with internal power and the rising of the ruling clan. From the 4th century onwards, they created strong ties with one of the Korean kingdoms, Baekje (Paekche in older transcriptions), which was located in the southern tip of the Korean Peninsula. As Baekje was threatened by the other two Korean kingdoms at the time, it started relying on military assistance of Yamato to preserve its independence. This escalated in the first half of the 5th century CE when Yamato invaded Silla, one of the other two Korean kingdoms, and for a short period, Baekje became dependent on Yamato. Baekje's crown prince was even sent to the Yamato court as a hostage to ensure this relation. It is in this period that Yamato reopened relations with China, sending ten diplomatic envoys to the court of the Liu Song dynasty by the end of the 5th century. It is likely that the Yamato kings did this on the advice of their Korean ally, as the Korean kingdoms had much closer ties with China than Japan in the previous centuries. These ties, especially the fact that the Yamato forces were involved to some degree in wars between Korean kingdoms, showcase how powerful this Japanese kingdom had become, evolving into a small regional power at the very least.

One of the reasons it became so powerful was due to trade, most notably with Baekje. But cultural ties were also created, allowing for Korean and Chinese influence on Yamato to grow, bringing various new technologies and knowledge. Most notable and important was writing, as it is during this period that the Japanese started to adopt and learn Chinese characters, which became the first script they used. At first, they were used to carve out symbols on swords, so the elite could demonstrate their supremacy. But literate immigrants became more and more appreciated by the nobles who saw the worth of the written word, slowly learning this important skill themselves. These contacts also refined rice cultivation and ironworking and brought horses to Japan. Because of this last fact, there were some theories that Yamato was actually conquered and ruled by one of the horse-riding peoples of the Asian plains, explaining its growth in power, but so far, no actual evidence for this has been found. Beside technologies, in the 5th century, the Yamato kingdom also started to accept two rather important ideologies from the Asian mainland. First was a centralized imperial government based on the Chinese model, which would improve the efficiency and power of the state. The other was Buddhism, which spread over East Asia from India. Both of these proved to be rather important for the future development of Japanese civilization.

But at the end of the 5th century, the power of Yamato started to fade as turmoil in its own territories started to erupt. It is possible that expensive expeditions in Korea, which did possibly result in some type of proto-colonial territorial gains, slowly weakened the central court as several other clans rose to prominence challenging the authority of Yamato kings. After several losses in Korea, resulting in the loss of all influence there by 540 CE and a failed rebellion in Kyushu in the 530s, it became clear that the kingdom of Yamato lost its previous power. It is at this time that its kings and court decided it was time to learn from the foreigners, to adapt their knowledge and ideas and strengthen their own position. With that, the Kofun period came to an end, but the foundation of imperial Japan was set and ready to blossom in the next several centuries.

Chapter 2 – Birth of Imperial Japan and Its Culture

As the old state system was showing its weaknesses, the Yamato kings realized the time for change was ripe. They looked at how foreigners, at this period the Chinese and Koreans, organized and headed their governments, and they started to implement a series of reforms that would essentially transform Yamato from a kingdom to an imperial state with an emperor on its throne. This centralization of state and culture is also evident in the name of this period, today called Asuka. It was named so in the 19th century after the new central region of the Yamato court, which was still in the Nara prefecture but several miles to the south of the old court center. That fact is a clear sign that the Yamato state was becoming increasingly centralized, and the first step toward this centralization was the expansion of the royal domain which began in the 530s CE.

This change was clearly influenced by the failed rebellion in Kyushu, as the Yamato kings realized that the power they accumulated from the royal lands situated around the court, which were directly controlled and owned by the royal family, wasn't sufficient anymore. To expand their strength and influence and regain their authority over their dependents and subjects, they had to enlarge their estate. So, the Yamato rulers started to create new estates, this time far away from the court in more remote regions that had important economic and strategic positions. These were managed by governors who directly answered to the king and whose positions weren't hereditary. This was important as it reaffirmed the reign of the Yamato rulers in lands that were farther away from their central region while at the same time creating new sources of income and military strength they needed to recuperate after the losses in Korea and the Kyushu rebellion. Further steps were also taken to increase the power of the royal clan. In the mid-6th century, around 560, Yamato rulers started to register and keep records of the households on their own estates. This practice facilitated easier tax collection and military drafts if needed, which further boosted the control of the Yamato kings. And later on, this policy was enforced throughout the entire Japanese territory.

The Yamato rulers didn't stop at increasing the level of control over only their domain. They also pursued the creation of districts, headed by district supervisors, which answered directly to the court. Districts were set up on lands that didn't belong to the royal family but to one of the subject clans in an attempt to create local governments that would strengthen the grip of the Yamato court over the lands that nominally wasn't theirs. Sometimes these supervisors were members or even heads of the local clans, but they were acting according to the commands of the central government. This was the basis of the bureaucratic regime that was created in the next century, increasing the need and importance of scribes. These changes in the administrative system were facilitated by the new wave of immigrants from Korea, which also provided the central government with the educated personnel it needed. It was a trade of a sort, as Baekje needed further military assistance, but Yamato was reluctant to help as it proved too costly in the past. To appease the Japanese kings, the Koreans sent their scholars and scribes to the Yamato court. In return, the Yamato kings sent them military supplies and, in some cases, armed forces as well but only if the circumstances were opportune.

Map of the expansion of Yamato. Source: https://commons.wikimedia.org

The question of relations between Yamato and Baekje divided Japanese society, or at least the noble class. Some of the court ministers thought that sending more soldiers abroad was futile, while others saw benefit from those military expeditions. This led to a series of political clashes between some of the leading noble clans in 540. The result of these clashes was the rise to prominence of the Soga clan, which from this point onwards played an important role in early Japanese history. It was one of the first clans to achieve its major political breakthrough, not through war and martial success, but rather through methods of production and administration imported from Korea and China. And with guidance from the Soga clan head, the Yamato court adopted the policy of focusing government actions on accumulating both wealth and control, similar to the 19th-century

Japanese motto "Rich country, strong army." As such, the actions in Korea weren't completely halted but were more carefully evaluated to maximize their gains. As this policy proved successful, the Soga clan's influence rose, with their head becoming the top minister in the court with the title of the great royal chieftain. The Soga clan even intermarried with the royal family several times, becoming Japan's leading gaiseki (in-law) clan. Their power grew so much that they practically ruled over Yamato, despite the royal family sitting on the throne. It was a precedent that would become a regular practice in Japanese history through the institution of the shōgunate.

Closer relations between Baekje and Japan, combined with the rise of the Soga clan, gave birth to one more important novelty, today rather synonymous with Japanese civilization. That is Buddhism, which arose in India around the 5th century BCE and traveled through China and Korea, where it arrived around the 3rd century CE, to Japan in the mid-6th century. According to traditional sources, the first missionaries were sent by the Baekje court as sort of a present to the Yamato king. It is disputable if this was the case or if the transfer of Buddhism started naturally with migration, but whatever was the case, Japanese opposed the new religion vigorously at first. But the Soga clan, who had adopted other Chinese ideas and technologies, supported it. And after several decades, when they became the ruling power in the state, Buddhism gained royal support from the prince regent Shōtoku, and his aunt, Empress Suiko, both born of Soga mothers. Buddhism for them was imperishably connected with the civilizational development and ideas that came from China and Korea, so the Soga supported this new religion as well. For them, it was a sign of cultural advancement. And with acceptance of Buddhism, ideas of Confucianism, Taoism, and general Chinese thought flowed into Japan. It was the start of the so-called Asuka enlightenment, which bore a recognizable Buddhist characteristic at its core.

Prince Shōtoku played a crucial role in that, as he wrote the Seventeen-article constitution in 604 CE which heavily borrowed from the Confucian ideals of harmony and value in society. It wasn't a constitution in the modern sense of the word but more of a guideline for the behavior and morals of government officials. He also introduced a cap-ranking system in the Yamato court where the ranks of government officials would be differentiated by the color of their hats, a tradition found in the Chinese state system. In 600, Shōtoku and Suiko sent an envoy to the newly united Chinese empire, the first direct contact between the two countries after more than a century. This newly opened relationship only furthered Chinese cultural influence on Yamato. But reports of this Japanese envoy show another development in the Yamato court. Empress Suiko's representative introduced her to the Chinese emperor as the great queen (okimi), which was a traditional Yamato title that emphasized her relation to heaven, in a way imitating the Chinse imperial ideology that calls their emperor "the Son of Heaven." This signaled to the Chinese court that the Yamato rulers started to see themselves as equal to their emperors and they were angered by that, which soured further Sino-Japanese relations a bit. This shows that imperial ideology was starting to form in Japan, clearly influenced once again by Chinese traditions.

These political developments in Japan were further showed in 607 when a new envoy was sent to China. It seems that Suiko was referred to as tenshi, "the Child of Heaven." The parallel to the Chinese imperial ideology was apparent, but officially, it wasn't until the beginning of the late 7th or early 8th century that the Japanese rulers used their imperial title, tennō (heavenly emperor), for the first time. After they changed their title, official histories called all members of the Yamato dynasty emperors and empresses, even those who ruled in earlier centuries. In the earliest Japanese histories, they also promoted the connection of their dynasty with the gods. Emperors and empresses were descendants of the goddess Amaterasu, with the mythical first emperor, Jimmu, being her great-great-great-grandson. According to Yamato dynasty traditions, he ruled from 660 to 585 BCE, forming the state of Yamato itself. Modern historians have disregarded this as only legend, tracing the earliest possible historical ruler of Yamato to be the 15th emperor named Ōjin who traditionally ruled from 270 to 310 CE. And the tradition of calling the rulers of the Yamato dynasty tennō survived to modern times, and in most histories, those early kings and queens, like Suiko, are still referred to with imperial titles.

Prince Shōtoku and his two sons. Source: https://commons.wikimedia.org

With the diplomatic envoy of 607, Prince Shōtoku sent more than just the Yamato court representatives. He also sent a number of young men to be educated in Chinese schools and universities. This was another wise move done by him and Empress Suiko, as those men were going to head the second wave of reforms in the mid-7th century. But before they were to arrive back home, political upheaval shook the royal court. By the end of the 620s, both Suiko and Shōtoku had died, as well as the old Soga clan chief. As the Soga clan had heavily intermarried with the royal dynasty, the matter of succession became a matter in which the new head of the Soga clan interfered, trying to maximize his influence. He and other members of the Soga clan who held high court ranks started to abuse their power. This antagonized other nobles, even some distant branches of the Soga clan. As the years went by, new issues of regal succession arose, once again meddled with by the Soga chief. Finally, it was too much for the opposition, and a coup d'état was organized by Prince Naka no Ōe, the future emperor Tenji, and Fujiwara no Kamatari, founder of the Fujiwara clan. The Soga were accused of trying to grab the throne for themselves, and their most prominent leaders were killed.

After the coup, the new ruler of Yamato became Prince Naka's uncle, Emperor Kōtoku. Prince Naka no Ōe became the head of state affairs, similar to the position of Prince Shōtoku. Fujiwara no Kamatari became their chief advisor, with two more high-ranking nobles acting as government ministers. They also appointed the scholars that were sent by Prince Shōtoku to China, who had returned to Japan during the 640s, to serve in the government, as they possessed precious knowledge of the Chinese state system. With their help, Prince Naka and Fujiwara further transformed the Japanese administrative and legal system, continuing the Soga path of implementing Chinese ideas. These changes became known as the Taika (Great Change) Reforms, which unfolded over several decades and resulted in the final transformation of the old royal system into the new imperial system. The first action taken by Emperor Kōtoku and Prince Naka was to have all the ministers swear an oath to the ruler, asserting the principle that a sovereign and his advisers were to rule the state directly and not the prominent chieftains of powerful clans.

In the next few years, the central government under Prince Naka and Fujiwara continued to enact new measures aimed to increase the power and authority of the central government. They nationalized the lands, abolishing the clans' hereditary possession of lands, and then used the repossessed property to materially support government officials if needed. The government also took over the direct control of Buddhist temples from the clans, appointing their own priests. This was done to decrease the symbolic strength of the clans. With further reforms, they surveyed the lands and people to facilitate the collection of existing taxes as well as forming new ones. Most levies were now paid based on production, roughly 3% of the yield. But fixed taxes existed for houses and land, as well as weapons and horses. Furthermore, reformers seized weapons across the country, limiting rebellions by the discontent nobles. The entire country was divided into provinces, which were headed by government-appointed provincial inspectors. These provinces were further divided into districts with supervisors carrying out the imperial will. Below them were village heads, presiding over roughly fifty households and tasked with preventing and dealing with crime and enforcing the payment of taxes. Finally, imperial edicts proclaimed the allowed size of burial mounds for each class and rank, so even in death, one's place in the hierarchy could be known. All of the mentioned reforms undoubtedly show the direct imperial rule of the Yamato king over the state as well as the forming of the distinct hierarchical system.

Yet after several years, the spirit of reformation dwindled. The new system needed some time to work itself out and become fully functioning, and the reformists needed to replenish their energy. In 654, Emperor Kōtoku died and was succeeded by his sister. In that period, the Chinese empire, under the Tang dynasty, started to expand its influence in Korea and in 660 CE invaded the kingdom of Baekje, a traditional ally of the Yamato court. The Chinese were assisted by another Korean kingdom, Silla, and they managed to quickly crush the Baekje forces. Their leaders turned to Japan for help, but the Yamato expedition was delayed as the queen had died in the summer of 661. It was the right time for

Prince Naka to take his rightful place on the throne as Emperor Tenji. He heard the pleas of his allies and in 663 sent his armies across the sea to help restore Baekje, but they were no match for the combined Tang-Silla military. After this failure, Baekje became a semi-independent kingdom under the Tang protectorate, and Japan lost all of its influence in Korea. In the next couple of years, China attacked the third Korean kingdom called Koguryŏ, which was located in the northern area of the peninsula. They also tried to gain military assistance from Tenji, but he realized that at the moment Korea was out of the reach for his state.

Despite their failure, this military and political defeat shook up the Yamato court, and the reformistic spirit was once again fired up. It was rekindled both by fear of a Tang invasion, which led to increased construction of defensive structures and forts, as well as the influx of educated Korean immigrants from the fallen Baekje government. Those refugees, as we might call them today, brought with them knowledge which was used to increase the control and authority of the central administration, increase its income, and strengthen the Yamato economy in general. Tenji's government recognized the worth of those Korean scholars and nobles and gave them lower court ranks to help further the reforms. The first step in the reform process was to once again reappraise and increase the number of government ranks. Then, in 668 CE, the first administrative law, known as Ōmi-ryō, was issued. This legal code was certainly based upon the traditions of the Chinese bureaucratic system and philosophies of Confucianism. The exact contents of the Ōmi-ryō are unknown as it was lost to time. This fact made its entire existence questionable to some historians, but through circumstantial evidence, it was confirmed as real. And though it was most likely compiled by Fujiwara no Kamatari, it was certainly heavily influenced by the Korean-educated immigrants. The end result of these reforms was the increased strength of the

Yamato state in both internal and external affairs, driven by fear of a Chinese attack.

Later illustration of Emperor Tenji. Source:
https://commons.wikimedia.org

Yet no matter how much authority the state managed to accumulate, it was still vulnerable to internal dynastic struggles. In 672, Tenji died, leaving his son and brother to compete for the throne. For a few months, the civil war disrupted the reforms. From the fight, Tenji's brother, Tenmu, emerged as the new ruler. Some modern historians believe that before his ultimate victory, Tenji's son managed to be crowned, counting him in the list of Japanese emperors. But this remains disputable and less important, considering that even if it was true, his reign wasn't longer than a couple of months. By the time Tenmu solidified his place on the throne, Silla directly challenged the Chinese empire and by 668 managed to unify Korea. This meant that the threat to

Yamato wasn't coming from the Chinese anymore but from traditionally hostile Silla, which had now become a true international power. Looking at both Korean and Chinese state models, as well as Yamato traditions, Tenmu set out to further strengthen his rule by building what was to become known as tennō-sei, the Japanese imperial government system.

To achieve that, as well as to secure his country from a possible invasion, he first reformed and unified the military. He created an imperial army, stationing it in the remote regions and around the capital, and then incorporated local clans into that system by awarding them titles and ranks. Thus, he made every local chieftain into a loyal military commander, increasing the strength of the imperial army. This innovation transformed Yamato into a clan-based military state. Tenmu then proceeded to increase the unity and loyalty of his subjects by increasing his priestly and spiritual authority. He started to emphasize the connection between the royal family and Amaterasu, setting the ceremonial and institutional base of Yamato monarchs as the high priests or priestesses of kami worship, a religion which is also known as Shinto. Furthermore, he finalized and widened the process of the imperial throne taking over control of Buddhist temples. This gave the Yamato state more of a theocratic character, influenced by the policies of Silla kings. Finally, Tenmu once again reformed administrative divisions of Yamato, its central government, and revised the Ōmi-ryō, adding new laws to it. Despite the fact the revision was done three years after his death in 689, his legislative reforms advanced Yamato toward Chinese-styled bureaucratic order.

Tenmu's reforms were polished and completed by his grandson Monmu who, after a brief regent rule of Tenmu's wife, ascended to the throne in 697. He issued the Taihō-ritsuryō in 701 which, besides adding criminal law (Ritsu), finished the institutionalization of the imperial government. On top was the monarch, whose will was expressed through decrees (mikotonori) and edicts (semmy). Below him were the Department of Worship (Jingi-kan), tasked with religious matters, and the Department of State (Daijō-kan), which was occupied with secular issues. The Department of State was headed by the chancellor, who was the ruler's closest advisor and most trusted official. He was helped by Ministers of the Left and Right and four Great Councillors. All of them together were tasked with making important policy decisions. Below them were three Minor Councillors, Controllers of the Left and Right, as well as eight ministries, which fulfilled and enacted the will of the monarch and the high officials. The entire country was divided into eight regions, one of them being the capital. Those regions were further divided into provinces, which usually had at least one military corps of about a thousand men stationed in them. Below them were districts and then townships and villages. Of course, the Taihō code also dealt with matters like establishing a 30-rank system of court officials, land ownership, registration of the population, etc.

With the Taihō-ritsuryō, the Japanese imperial system was finished, transforming the old Yamato kingdom into a Japanese empire. This can be symbolically represented with two examples, one of them being the actual change of the name from Yamato to Japan during the late 7th century CE. Chinese scribes up until that point usually called Yamato Wa or Woguo, which was belittling the Japanese by denoting their state as "dwarf country" and them as "submissive people," despite the Yamato court trying to use the same symbol with the meaning of "harmony." So, in that period, the royal court decided that new symbols would be used, which literally translated means "root/origin of the sun," or how Westerners today more usually say, "the land of the rising sun." When those characters were read, they sounded like Nippon or Nihon, which is how the Japanese to this day call their country. So, it was at the end of the 7th century that Japan was born from Yamato, which remained the name of the imperial dynasty. The second example was the birth of the title tennō. It was first recorded in the two earliest histories written by the Japanese, Kojiki (c. 711) and Nihon Shoki (720), and in them, all previous rulers of Japan are denoted as emperors, even the mythical ones that predated the Yamato court. As they were largely written to give credit to the reforms and rules of both Tenmu and Monmu, historians argue that it was one of them who first chose the title for himself instead of it being attributed to them posthumously.

Extent of Japanese expansion by the time of the Taihō-ritsuryō.
Source: https://commons.wikimedia.org

With both of these facts, we can conclude that by 707 when Monmu died, the formation of the Japanese empire was both symbolically and factually finished without a doubt. It also roughly coincides with the end of the Asuka period, as Heijō-kyō (present-day city of Nara) became a new, proper capital, built with that sole purpose. But the state itself wasn't the only thing that went through a transformation and rebirth during that era. Influenced by

Chinese and Korean civilizations, Confucianism, Taoism, and mostly Buddhism, Japanese culture and society changed and evolved as well. The social structure still relied upon strict hierarchy and clan division, which is still synonymous with the Japanese even today, but it was now more based on imperial ranking and administrative division. And art forms such as paintings and sculptures were heavily influenced by the Chinese style and Buddhist traditions, and they started to resemble the traditional Japanese style as we envision it today. Other art forms, like literary works, were for the first time created in this period, as writing itself was first introduced in Japan by China in this era. It is when classical Japanese poetry, also known as Waka, was born. But despite the heavy foreign influences, Japanese civilization managed to preserve its uniqueness, which it possesses even today.

So, by 710 and the beginning of the so-called Nara period, named after the new capital, the almost two centuries long birth of imperial Japan and its culture was finished. The foundations were laid for the Japanese state and society, which remained in place until the 20th century. And the base of its civilization, through cultural proliferation and growth, are visible even in the 21st century in modern Japan. Yet there were even more achievements to be attained by the Japanese in the following centuries, as this was just the beginning of their empire and dynasty.

Chapter 3 – History of Classical Japan

The imperial state system, which was put in place by the end of the Asuka period, was the institutional creation of the Japanese empire. The use of the tennō title and the new country name was its symbolic representation. But the Yamato rulers realized that they also needed a more physical representation of that crucial change. Once again, they looked to the west, to the Chinese, for inspiration, as they chose to erect the first real and lasting capital in the present-day city of Nara, in the region of the same name. Giving the name to the period that followed, this city was modeled upon the rectangular grid pattern of the Chinese capital Chang'an (modern-day Xi'an). With the move of the capital to Nara, which began in 708 and was finished by 710 CE, the imperial regime had gained a more permanent government, economic, and cultural center, as well as a symbolic and tangible representation of its authority.

Before Emperor Monmu died, he expressed his will to have his mother succeed him until his son became old enough to assume the imperial position. So, in 707, she became Empress Genmei. Supporting her and acting as her highest advisor was Fujiwara no Fuhito, the son of Fujiwara no Kamatari, one of the leaders of the Taika Reforms. One of the first actions taken by the new empress was the aforementioned move of the capital, choosing Nara as the auspicious location as it was surrounded by mountains on three sides. She was also concerned about leaving her grandson a new and more imposing palace to rule from, which would represent their recently gained imperial authority. She wanted to support it with religious and spiritual signs of the monarchical grandeur, so Genmei ordered many new Buddhist temples to be built there, as well as moving and rebuilding older important temples. Thus, Nara became the holy center of the empire as well. Fuhito had his own reasons to support this change of capitals. First of all, the three mountains made this city safer and easier to defend. Secondly, it had a more direct connection via rivers to the Inland Sea harbor of Naniwa (present-day Osaka). This made its location economically more suitable and prosperous. Its rise as the political, economic, and spiritual center of a mighty empire became obvious as it quickly grew to 200,000 inhabitants, out of which between 7,000 and 10,000 were government officials, and covered an area of about 25 km^2 (9.65 mi^2).

But building such a city, with all of these astonishing building projects, took its toll on the state. It required a lot of funding and corvée labor, which is unpaid work done by the commoners for the state. The discovery of copper in the area near modern Tokyo and the subsequent mining of it proved to be an important boost for the Japanese economy, as metal was scarce in the archipelago. It increased production and decreased Japan's dependence on imports while at the same time facilitating local trade, as local copper was used to mint coins for the first time. But even that wasn't enough as surveys and reports show us that over 90% of the population was living in poverty or barely over it. In some regions, the percentages were even worse. It seems prosperity was limited to Nara and its surrounding districts, while any significant trade, production, or other economic aspects of life outside of the capital was almost at a standstill. Fuhito realized that this issue was rather important, and he tried to stimulate the economy by easing the transport of goods with post stations on the roads, lowering debt interests of the commoners, and preventing nobles from taking their lands. He also tried to make the local administrative system more efficient. Furthermore, the imperial government was spreading its control north, conquering new regions and people, while at the same time creating new arable land on its already existing territories.

Miniature model of the imperial palace in Heijō-kyō (Nara)
Source: https://commons.wikimedia.org

However, none of these methods and attempts were enough to make life in 8th-century Japan significantly any better. Fuhito was aware of this so in 717 he started to work on revising the old Taihō legal code, adding new laws to it. But he died a few months before it was finished in 720, so Yōrō-ritsuryō, as it was named, wasn't enacted until 757. Despite that, historians today think that his work on this code did, in fact, manage to reinforce administrative bureaucracy, as it endeavored to increase state revenue and control.

It would be easy to blame imperial thirst for proving its might through huge projects as the sole reason for economic despair. But internal struggles among the nobles and the imperial family also contributed to it. Most clan aristocrats were more involved in intrigues, court affairs, and the gathering of influence than in actually leading the country. The political turmoil began from the death of Monmu, as not all members of the elite supported Empress Genmei, Fujiwara no Fuhito, and their pretend to the throne, Prince Obito. Yet thanks to the prestige and power of the entire Fujiwara clan and Fuhito's personal influence, they managed to stay in control. Empress Genmei and Fuhito even managed to make Obito, Fuhito's grandson, a crown prince in 714.

For unknown reasons, Genmei stepped down from the throne in 715; however, Obito didn't succeed her. In a unique precedent, her own daughter, Empress Genshō, inherited the title. In previous centuries, it was rather common for women to become crowned rulers but only as regents. They would inherit the throne from a male member of the royal family and leave it to the rightful heir when he came of age. For this reason, it is today considered that the rule of empresses was only temporary, despite them being fully-fledged monarchs with the same authority and obligations as males. This reasoning was later used to proclaim that male-only inheritance was a tradition of the Yamato dynasty. In fact, after Genshō, it became rather rare for empresses to ascend to the throne. At this point in time, only three more women sat on the Japanese throne. Nonetheless, Genshō's reign was secured by Fuhito, who was the strongest political figure in the empire until his death in 720. With him gone, the Fujiwara clan lost their controlling grip on the government as one of the imperial princes instead became the most influential figure in court.

However, that "interregnum" of the Fujiwara clan was brief, lasting less than ten years. By the end of the 720s, the government fell back under the control of the Fujiwara, or more specifically, four of Fuhito's sons. The regime of the four Fujiwara sons realized quickly that the economy of the empire was deteriorating. So, in the early 730s, they halved the taxes, abolished conscription, and founded charitable institutions and infirmaries.

At the same time, Prince Obito, who became Emperor Shōmu in 724, began to express his Buddhist zeal, building a wide network of temples, employing more priests, and erecting statues of Buddha across the country. It is likely he did this to increase the spiritual authority of the throne. Despite that, he retained the imperial association with ancestral shrines and kami ceremonies, which is linked with the Shinto religion. The Buddhist zeal was only strengthened when a smallpox epidemic ravaged Japan between 735 and 737, killing somewhere between 1/4 and 1/3 of the entire population. Among the victims of this disease were the four Fujiwara brothers, as well as many other high-ranking officials. The Japanese empire was devastated both socially and economically. This urged Shōmu to pour even more state funding into Buddhist temples to appease the gods. As the Fujiwara clan lost its representatives, Tachibana no Moroe, a removed member of the Yamato imperial clan, rose as the new leader of the court. He was backed by several smaller clans that were opposed to the Fujiwara, but friction between the Fujiwara and anti-Fujiwara camps continued.

It seems that Shōmu and his empress were also slightly leaning toward the Fujiwara, as they were the emperor's in-law family. Instability finally broke out in open combat as the son of one of the four Fujiwara brothers rebelled in 740. The central government, under Moroe's direction, sent troops and quickly quelled the uprising. Fearing further revolts, the emperor decided to move his capital several times before going back to Nara in 745. In those years, Moroe's regime tried to dampen the effects of the smallpox epidemic with several policies such as lowering the number of officials appointed in local governments and simplifying the administrative system. They also banned private lending and decreased the number of conscripted soldiers. But the biggest and most important change was when the government allowed for any newly cleared pieces of land to remain in possession of the cultivator. This, in essence, undermined one of the essential ideas of the ritsuryō system which stated that all the land belonged to the emperor. It did slightly help the state income, but in the long run, it enabled the accumulation of private lands and degraded imperial power. However, in 745, Shōmu fell ill and decided to make his daughter who was born by a Fujiwara mother his successor as all his sons had died prematurely. In 749, the old emperor finally abdicated in favor of Empress Kōken, marking the beginning of Moroe's fall, which was neither quick nor easy. He continued to occupy a high-ranking position in the government for several years, though his influence started to waver.

Emperor Shōmu. Source: https://commons.wikimedia.org

At the same time, Fujiwara no Nakamaro, the new leader of the Fujiwara clan, started to increase his power and position in court, and eventually, Moroe was forced to resign in 756. The rift between the two factions was further widened when retired Emperor Shōmu died that very same year, which led to turmoil in the court. Moroe died in 757, and as the opposition was losing its foothold, Nakamaro was given a ministerial position which wasn't constituted by the ritsuryō. The anti-Fujiwara faction felt threatened and tried to organize a coup, but their plans were discovered and thwarted by the Fujiwara clan. That very year Nakamaro also finally enacted the Yōrō-ritsuryō, compiled by his famous predecessor Fuhito. His ruthlessness in dealing with the opposition lost him popularity among the people. He tried to alleviate that by cutting taxes and military services, expanding the empire to the north, and colonizing border regions in Honshu. It seems that despite his unpopularity his rule was remarkably strong as no one could challenge him.

In 758, Empress Kōken abdicated in favor of her distant cousin, Emperor Junnin, who was nothing but a mere puppet on the throne. Though details of her resignation are unclear, it is not unlikely that Nakamaro had some hand in it considering that soon afterward Kōken started to oppose him more directly. A turning point was the death of her mother and Nakamaro's chief ally in court in 760. This rift between them was furthered in two years when Kōken became close, possibly even intimate, with an elderly Buddhist mystical priest named Dōkyō. The two of them started to gather Nakamaro's opposition around them, including some disgruntled members of the Fujiwara clan. It was enough to make him feel threatened as in 764 he attempted a coup. In a battle, Nakamaro's forces were defeated, and he was killed. Within a year, Emperor Junnin was exiled while Kōken was placed on the throne again as Empress Shōtoku. She then proceeded to favor Dōkyō, giving him ranks and positions, even considering leaving the throne to him as she was unmarried and childless. But the Fujiwara clan, who despite the fall of Nakamaro remained the most prominent one, didn't allow this to happen. So, after

Shōtoku (Kōken) died in 770, they chose an obscure member of the imperial family, the grandson of Emperor Tenji, who lacked any considerable political ambition. He became known as Emperor Kōnin.

Under his rule, the Fujiwara clan continued to exert supreme control over the state. They cut down the number of administrative officials, shifted conscription more toward the rich, and became harsher toward criminals. In 781, Kōnin's son succeeded him as Emperor Kanmu. Early in his rule, he was a target of a failed coup led by other members of the imperial family, so he and his Fujiwara allies decided to move the capital from Nara in 784. The Fujiwara clan backed this decision because they felt it could control emperors easier in a new capital. Kanmu also sought to leave as Buddhist monks, thanks to the state-backed religion policy, grew too powerful and influential, endangering the throne itself as was seen in the case of Dōkyō. Thus, the Nara period had ended, paradoxical as it was. On the one hand, it was a time of great state projects, the building of an impressive city, and the spreading of culture in general. But on the other, it was a time of poverty and death, political turmoil and intrigues, without much splendor and dazzle. But on whatever side of the coin we decide to focus on, it was a period in which Japanese culture and history entered its classical era, marking how that civilization would develop in future centuries.

Emperor Kanmu chose Nagaoka-kyō, located 32 km (20 mi) northwest of Nara, in an area which was suitably located for land and water communication, even better than Nara. But it was surrounded by marshes and prone to flooding. In 785, the emperor's chief advisor and ally from the Fujiwara clan was assassinated in Nagaoka-kyō by clans that opposed the move and the Fujiwara in general. The leader of this opposition was the emperor's brother, Sawara, who felt endangered by Fujiwara influence. Sawara was exiled, but he presumably chose death instead. Soon famine, devastating floods, and widespread disease hit the city. Kanmu realized he had to move his capital once again, so he chose Heian-kyō (modern-day Kyoto) in 794. Thus, the Heian period began, marking the pinnacle of Japanese classical civilization. The beginning of this era was somewhat an exception in Japanese history. Most emperors before and after Kanmu were largely dependent on great clans, like the Fujiwara, being more in charge of spiritual affairs and acting as a symbol of Japanese unity. But Kanmu was different, and in that aspect, he might have been the greatest emperor in pre-modern Japanese history.

Miniature model of Heian-kyō (modern-day Kyoto).
Source: https://commons.wikimedia.org

Kanmu became an emperor as an adult who was well educated and an experienced court official. Raised with Confucian tradition in mind, he lacked the Buddhist zeal of his predecessors and wasn't keen on spending state money on building extravagant temples. Instead, he was a rather pragmatic monarch. Circumstances around the time of his reign also helped his independent rule. Lesser clans filled several roles in the Department of State after the government crisis in the 770s, and with the last great Fujiwara leader assassinated in 785, Kanmu personally saw that no new chiefs from powerful clans would fill any important government office. Instead, he put his own relatives from the imperial house in those positions or left them vacant. He also allied with smaller clans to counter any opposition from the major ones. Kanmu was also aided by the two moves of the capital as it was expensive for clans to move so often, which made it harder for them to focus on gaining positions in court. In the end, though not an absolute sovereign, his word was indeed final in the empire, giving him power that few emperors in Japan held.

Emperor Kanmu. Source: https://commons.wikimedia.org

Some of his most notable achievements were the further conquests and colonization in the northeastern parts of Honshu against the Emishi people. They were rather primitive chiefdoms; some of them were in agricultural societies, and others were hunter-gatherer groups. Their exact origins are unknown, though some have suggested they may have been linked with the Ainu people who currently live in Hokkaido, although no clear evidence for that has been found. The Japanese have described them as hairy barbarians of the north, and despite their savagery, they were respected as fierce warriors. Prior to the rule of Emperor Kanmu, some of their tribes were conquered, which led to an uprising in the late 770s, for which Kanmu planned retribution in 781. And despite all of the advantages of the Japanese empire, the first three campaigns against the Emishi ended either as defeats or at best inconclusively. For over two decades, the northern borders of Japan were under constant threat of Emishi attacks until 802 when the imperial army managed to inflict a major defeat to the barbarians. This victory extended and consolidated Japanese rule in the northern part of Honshu. The 38-year-long Emishi war was concluded inconclusively in 811, five years after Kanmu's death, with a limited victory of another Japanese expedition.

Yet this war and victory, no matter how limited it was, became more important for Japanese society than mere territorial expansion. Constant wars waged mostly by eastern Honshu provinces caused the creation of private warrior forces. They became the forerunners of the future warrior class that is so synonymous with the Japanese culture. Adding to that was relocating groups of Emishi people to the south as part of the colonizing tactics. Though many of those communities quickly perished, some managed to assimilate. Those that managed to survive brought their warlike skills to the Japanese culture, becoming possible ancestors of warrior families throughout Japan. But this long and tough campaign was rather expansive, and together with the cost of building a new capital, it put a huge strain on state finances. That is why in 805 Kanmu halted further constructions in Heian as well as further campaigns against the Emishi. He tried to relieve the pressure on his treasury by eliminating unneeded administrative offices, tightening the control of the local provincial governments, and adjusting taxes. Kanmu even cut down expenses for the upkeep of members of the dynasty by excluding imperial descendants in the fifth generation and after from the royal clan.

Fiscal responsibility was also a characteristic of his eldest son and successor Emperor Heizei who ascended to the throne in 806. This made him rather unpopular among the nobility, who also disliked his scandal-prone behavior. But in 810, he became gravely ill, so he abdicated in favor of his younger brother Emperor Saga. However, soon after his retirement, Heizei moved to Nara and with the help of one part of the Fujiwara clan tried to rebel against Saga. Their plans were thwarted, and Heizei was sent to a Buddhist monastery while the rebellious Fujiwara were exiled. Saga himself became the pillar of imperial rule, as he inherited his father's erudition and his skill in administration. He abdicated in favor of his brother Emperor Junna in 823 but remained a vital force behind the dynastic authority as he retained a lot of power and influence. Until his death in 842, Fujiwara influence in the court was limited, which meant the Japanese monarch managed to retain their authority. Their limited influence at court was partially intentional as Saga was careful not to create strong martial connections with them and to avoid giving too many Fujiwara high-ranking offices. He also created a clan consisting of former imperial family members named Minamoto (sometimes called Genji) which also served as a counterweight to the Fujiwara clan. But the Fujiwara helped as well in this loss of power as they themselves broke off into several houses which fought amongst themselves for power, decreasing their influence in the court.

Emperor Saga. Source: https://commons.wikimedia.org

Saga's influence was powerful enough to guide the imperial house through another abdication, as in 833 Junna gave up the throne in favor of Emperor Ninmyō. As Saga's son, he obeyed his father by promoting Junna's son as his crown prince and successor. During the first half of the 9th century, despite all the efforts of Saga and Junna to adapt the ritsuryō system to newly developing social and economic circumstances, the central government was slowly losing its control. This trend was helped by the fact that the nobles and imperial family members were slowly starting to accumulate private land through grants or cultivation of new parcels. So, when Saga died in 842, the Yamato dynasty lost their much-needed and capable leader who managed to preserve imperial rule. Within weeks, the royal court was split into two factions. The crown prince, Junna's son, felt that his position was in danger. Both Junna and Saga were dead, so he, rightfully it seems, presumed that Ninmyō was about to place his own son as his successor instead of him. So, backed by several important nobles, including some of the imperial line and Fujiwara clan, he plotted a coup. The emperor caught wind of his intentions and acted preemptively. The crown prince was deposed and replaced by Ninmyō's son, the future Emperor Montoku, while several leading nobles were demoted or exiled.

This event marked a return of Fujiwara influence on the court as the new crown prince was born by a Fujiwara mother and was a nephew of Fujiwara no Yoshifusa, a powerful noble who was on the rise at the time. Ninmyō passed away in 850 and was succeeded by Emperor Montoku, who was now heavily influenced by Yoshifusa and his Northern House branch of Fujiwara. Yoshifusa took the opportunity to marry his daughter to the new monarch, and she became the mother of the future Emperor Seiwa. Yoshifusa also promoted his kinsmen to government offices, and ultimately in 857, he himself became the Chancellor (Daijō-daiji), the highest office in the government. Within a year, Montoku died, and Yoshifusa's grandson became the new emperor. Through this, his position was further solidified as he became Seiwa's regent, a position which was officially recognized in 866 when he was awarded the title of sesshō (regent). As the years went by, Yoshifusa purged the court of his political opponents, and by the time of his death in 872, his prestige and sway over state affairs were greater than any noble in the past. In essence, he became an emperor without a crown or a throne.

But as he couldn't have his own son, Yoshifusa adopted his brother's son, which was a common practice at the time. His adopted heir, Fujiwara no Mototsune, continued in his footsteps. He became the regent of seven-year-old Emperor Yōzei in 876 when Seiwa abdicated. Yōzei grew to be a rather violent person, with many comparing him to the famously cruel Roman Emperor Caligula, with some stories implicating him in murders of some courtiers. So, in 884, Mototsune forced him to abdicate, choosing the elderly Emperor Kōkō as his successor. This was an exception in the Fujiwara policy of choosing underage emperors as they were easier to control, making it easier for that clan to retain its grip over the court. It is possible that he was chosen to restore some of the imperial prestige lost with Yōzei's viciousness. Kōkō's son Uda inherited the throne in 887 after his father died. During the next year, Mototsune was awarded the newly created title of kampaku ("internuncio"), with which he and all later holders of the title became the regents of the adult emperors. The Yamato dynasty could do little about this but watch as they lost their control over the country. This precedent meant the Fujiwara regency was fully established, making them more important and influential than the emperors themselves, as imperial authority declined and their position became merely symbolic. It is worth noting that it is mostly because of this that the practice from the Nara and Asuka periods of sisters and mothers acting as regents was lost. That tradition was used to prevent the dissolution of imperial authority from the Yamato dynasty, but the Fujiwara clearly had no use for that practice as they themselves were the ones who usurped the power.

Unfortunately for the Fujiwara clan, in 891 Mototsune died without leaving a competent heir. That gave Uda some room to restore imperial power, opting to rely on the nobility of a middle rank which had fewer ties with the Fujiwara. One of them was Sugawara no Michizane, a provincial governor who was a scholar-official, a bureaucrat specially educated for administrative positions who had in-depth understandings of issues that troubled the government. He rose to become Minister of the Right, which was unprecedented for a noble of his rank. But as a pragmatic bureaucrat, he advocated for reworking the statutory code, adjusting it to the new circumstances in local administration.

Michizane realized from his own experiences that governors were unable to fulfill their tasks properly as the ritsuryō system was falling apart with the rise of provincial gentry with large properties, growth of the vagrant population, and the distortion of population registers. Despite the soundness of his proposals, Michizane's ideas were rejected. His position was weakened when Uda abdicated in favor of his son, Daigo, who became the new emperor in 897. By that time, Fujiwara no Tokihira, Mototsune's son, had matured enough to clash with Michizane in a scramble for power. Tokihira proved to be a better politician, managing to persuade young Daigo that Uda and Michizane had conspired against him. For that, Michizane was demoted and exiled. Yet Tokihira's victory was short as he himself died in 909, leaving once again the Fujiwara clan without a strong chief.

For the remainder of his rule, Daigo managed to reign without much interference of the Fujiwara, though their presence in the court was still substantial. Tadahira, the new Fujiwara leader, did manage to secure the position of crown prince to an emperor's son born by a Fujiwara mother, which was crucial for the return of Fujiwara influence. In 930, Emperor Daigo died, and he was succeeded by his 7-year-old son and Tadahira's nephew, Emperor Suzaku. Tadahira became his regent and in 941 took the title of kampaku when Suzaku became an adult. And until 949, when Tadahira died, the three highest offices were held by the Fujiwara—to be more precise, Tadahira and his brothers or sons. The country was once again in the firm grip of the Fujiwara. During the 940s, the central government finally realized it had to adapt to the changing economic and social circumstances. The government instituted land taxes in place of per capita taxation. It also accepted private land ownership, though it tried to limit its expansion, and it recognized local governments as quasi-autonomous units. Provincial governors from that point had only contractual tax obligations, which meant that instead of fixed levies, their financial duties to the central government were changing every year depending on economic circumstances. This weakened the power of the central government, eroding what was left of the ritsuryō system. Thus, modern historians often call this new forming system the "Royal-Court State," distinguishing it from the older statutory regime.

Emperor Daigo. Source: https://commons.wikimedia.org

These changes weren't abrupt; they were merely formal recognitions of practices that took root over the years. Yet the decline of the central government's authority was obvious. In the late 930s, a large landowner and descendent of Emperor Kanmu rebelled and proclaimed himself as the new emperor in the eastern provinces. At the same time, piracy became a problem in the Inland Sea to the west. The central government managed to suppress these threats, but the eastern rebellion pointed toward future developments where local chiefs and their private warrior bands, created through family alliances and mutual local interests, would combat for their own goals. This was shaped into a full-blown samurai warrior society in the 11th and 12th centuries. In 946, Suzaku abdicated, being succeeded by his own brother, Emperor Murakami. From that point onwards, Fujiwara chiefs were the ones who not only held all real power, leaving emperors only as symbolic and religious leaders of the empire, but also were the ones who chose the line of succession. From 967, the office of regent became permanent, lasting for about 100 years and entrenching the Fujiwara clan as the actual rulers of Japan.

Within that century of Fujiwara regency, their authority was pretty much unrivaled as they enthroned and dethroned emperors at will. Political frictions and intrigues were mostly between the Fujiwara clan members. In the late 10th century, the government did try to stabilize the economy, steadying the supply of currency and prices while regulating the growth of private properties which were excluded from taxes. Yet these attempts were mostly in vain.

Contrary to governmental and imperial erosion, Japan's culture was flourishing. During the Heian period, Japan was slowly limiting its contact with China and Korea. Fewer and fewer envoys were being sent, and trade became their only connection. This was caused partially by the decline and fall of the Tang dynasty in China, which led to a decline in Chinese cultural influence in Japan, allowing for more indigenous artistic expression. This was seen in literature with examples in poetry as well as in new styles like novels and epics, which became rather popular in the court circles and among the higher nobles. Even the lyrics of the modern Japanese national anthem were written in this period. This "Japanization" is also evident in paintings where the Yamato style grew more popular. It is recognizable by the vivid colors and imagery of court life and religious stories of shrines and temples. But the most important cultural innovation was the development of kana, the original Japanese syllabic scripts, which are still being used today. It was easier to use and had much fewer symbols, though they were rooted in the Chinese script. Despite this innovation, literacy was still low, limited only to nobles and Buddhist clergy.

In contrast to the cultural advancements, the economy was further declining. Trade became limited as roads were largely guarded, and it regressed to the barter system as the government slowly stopped minting coins. On the other hand, the aristocratic elite continued to amass wealth through their private tax-exempt properties known as shōen. And as the number of shōen grew, the power of the central government fell. In the 1040s, the Fujiwara government tried to reform the economy, mostly to increase imperial income. Those reforms led to the state revenue becoming stabilized, but it recognized a large number of shōen estates, limiting the tax base even further. In turn, this gave local landowners and nobles a looser hand, eroding imperial authority even more. It seems that the Fujiwara clan, as well as other court nobles, were more preoccupied with their own affairs, intrigues, and struggles for influence rather than the welfare of the entire state. It should be noted, though, that the ministers were indeed working on everyday governmental issues, those were pushed aside when politics demanded it.

With that, by the mid-11th century, Japan was slowly entering the transition between the classical era, marked by a central government, real imperial authority, and a statutory system, and the medieval period. There, the emperors would become purely symbolic rulers in a country divided between clans, backed by the warrior samurai class, constantly locked in a fight for power and supremacy. But the cultural achievements of the classical era influenced future developments of Japanese civilization, often regarded by later generations as the Japanese golden age.

Chapter 4 – Early Medieval Japan

As the Fujiwara regency was coming to an end, Japan was on the brink of change. The rise of local landowners, backed by their armies, gave rise to a strong military class. As the struggle for power started to shift from court intrigues to open combat, the importance of this class was increasing. This was the birth of the samurai class, who dominated pretty much every aspect of life in Japan for centuries to come, giving the Japanese society a very recognizable form for which it is known today. Yet this transformation wasn't quick or straightforward. And before the emperors lost any trace of their real political authority, the royal clan tried for one last time to reinstate their control over their own empire.

Like many other historical events, this one was also largely shaped by chance. In 1068, Go-Sanjō became the 71ˢᵗ emperor of Japan. His ascension to the throne came at the point when Fujiwara might was on a sharp decline, losing its tight grip on the court. Despite their attempts, they weren't able to block Sanjō's enthronement, so for the first time since Emperor Uda, the Japanese monarch wasn't born by a Fujiwara mother. And more importantly, Sanjō was an adult, having served as crown prince for over 20 years, and he was determined to rule on his own. Being well educated in the Chinese style of ruling, which was based on a direct imperial rule, Go-Sanjō was determined to undermine the power of the highest-ranking nobles. He started to appoint middle-ranking nobles to higher governmental positions while at the same time turning toward the Minamoto imperial clan to replace Fujiwara in the Council of State. Emperor Go-Sanjō also tried to regulate shōen estates by creating the Records Office (kirokusho) which had to enforce his edicts that stipulated all estates created after 1045 or which had improper documentation should be declared illegal and confiscated, those lands later becoming private holdings of the imperial house. This, of course, was also aimed at decreasing the power of elite clans, chiefly the main house of Fujiwara. He also instated several economic reforms trying to standardize measurements, the quality of silk and hemp, and prices, all in an attempt to increase the income of the imperial treasury.

From all that, it would seem his reign would be long and prosperous, but that wasn't the case. He abdicated in 1073, after only five years of ruling. His eldest son became Emperor Shirakawa, while his younger son was named crown prince who was to succeed Shirakawa according to his father's wishes. Yet Sanjō died within months of his abdication, leaving his ambitious eldest son to rule as he wished. In many aspects, Emperor Shirakawa was just like his father, ruling directly, bypassing the Fujiwara and other high nobles' interference through his own authority, and by relying on the Minamoto clan and middle-ranked aristocrats. Fate pushed him to deviate from his father's plans as his half-brother died from a smallpox epidemic in 1085. Shirakawa then promoted his own son to that position, instead of his other half-brother, abdicating in 1087 to confirm his new succession line. He retired to a magnificent palace south of Heian and for a short period wasn't active in politics, though his personal authority prevented Fujiwara regents from dominating over his underage son, Emperor Horikawa, a kind, cautious, and devoted ruler. Despite these characteristics, he is remembered as more of a figurehead for his father, despite the fact that Shirakawa at that time was only passively present in the political life of the empire.

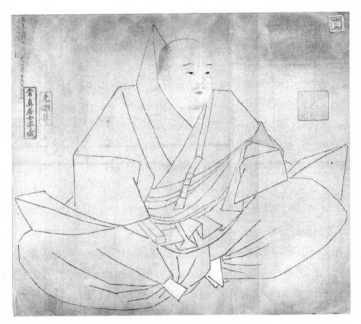

Emperor Shirakawa. Source: https://commons.wikimedia.org

But when Horikawa died in 1107 with a 4-year-old son as his successor, Shirakawa had no choice but to place himself in power again. Thus, he finalized the creation of the insei system of government, where the abdicated ex-emperor serves as the real sovereign behind the current emperor, preventing outside regency from eroding imperial authority. He achieved this through the in-no-chō, the private office of retired emperors. Though many historians link the creation of the insei system to Go-Sanjō, he died too early after his abdication to assert any pressure on Shirakawa. But he did lay the foundations on which Shirakawa himself erected the insei system. Creating this system allowed Shirakawa to prevent his half-brother and his descendants to jeopardize his own imperial line of succession through his grandson, Emperor Toba. Later on, in 1123, Shirakawa forced 20-year-old Toba to abdicate in favor of his son. Shirakawa probably did that to ensure his own control over the court, as Toba was growing up to be a rather capable ruler, more similar to him than to Horikawa. Emperor Sutoku succeeded him, and for the first six years of his rule, he was completely dominated by Shirakawa. But in 1129, Shirakawa finally died, leaving a power vacuum. Ex-emperor Toba filled it almost immediately, finally realizing his own desires for a direct rule and affirming the insei system.

Toba's policies were almost completely different from his grandfather. He made peace with the higher nobles, creating his personal retainers from some of them, and supported the idea of shōen as he gathered estates for himself. The only similarity between Shirakawa and Toba was their devotion to Buddhism and temple building. Toba had also gathered significant military strength as daily life in Japan became ever more dangerous. After the war, the central government waged against the once again rebelling Emishi in the 1050s onward, there were more and more local unrests and clan disputes. The weakened central government also proved to be a fertile ground for robbers and pirates. Ex-emperor Toba countered that problem by making Taira no Tadamori, the leading chief of a warrior band, his own retainer. By the mid-12th century, it became obvious that military clans, or branches dedicated to war, were becoming rather powerful and important as Tadamori was given treatment that a high noble would receive, despite being from a lesser class. But these noble warriors were still seen as retainers, as evident by their name samurai which means "one who serves." So, many other nobles looked at them with despise. But for the ex-emperor, they were a perfect ally to pacify his opponents.

By 1142, Toba decided to force his son Emperor Sutoku to abdicate in favor of his favorite and youngest son, Emperor Konoe, who at the time was only three years old. It was partially because he disliked Sutoku as the choice of Shirakawa, but there were also rumors that Sutoku was actually Shirakawa's son. Nevertheless, Konoe died in 1155 without producing an heir. Thus, Toba was forced to enthrone his middle son, Go-Shirakawa, despite thinking he wasn't fit to be a ruler. But before he could do anything else, he died in 1156. That left Go-Shirakawa under tremendous pressure from his brother Sutoku, which ended in a battle less than a month after Toba's death. Both brothers had backing from some members of the Fujiwara clan, giving them political influence, and parts of the Minamoto and Taira clans, giving them military power. The battle ended with Go-Shirakawa's victory and Sutoku's exile. He continued to rule for the next three years, trying to restore the symbolic importance of the throne by rebuilding the imperial palace, which had burned down in previous years, while also battling the issues of improperly gained shōen estates and illegal activities of the major Buddhist temples, such as pillaging and extortion, which plagued the commoners around them. In 1158, he abdicated in favor of his son while retaining his influence as an ex-emperor, continuing the path of the insei government set by his predecessors.

But his own son, Emperor Nijō, pushed back against his insei authority. He was fully aware that Toba wanted him to succeed; however, the old emperor thought it was unseemly to bypass Go-Shirakawa and enthrone his young son. Thus, Nijō did expect to be given autonomous control over the state when he arose on the throne. And he had significant support in his favor in the court. This animosity was increased by a Buddhist monk named Shinzei who worked closely with Go-Shirakawa to reach higher positions in the court, aiming to restore the idealized glorious past. This caused the so-called Heiji rebellion of the anti-insei forces in 1160, but it ended in their defeat. Despite that, Go-Shirakawa gained little by this as Shinzei also lost his life in the skirmish. And so, a struggle for power through political intrigue between father and son continued until 1165 when Nijō died, leaving his infant son to rule. Despite this victory, Go-Shirakawa wasn't as all-dominating as Toba or Shirakawa. His military ally from the Heiji rebellion, Taira no Kiyomori, gained a high office in the government after suppressing the revolt. Thus, he became an important political figure as well as a military leader and grew too influential, proving to be a challenge despite being more of a friend than a foe.

In 1168, Go-Shirakawa arranged the abdication of the infant emperor in favor of his own son, who became Emperor Takakura. This complicated the relationship between Go-Shirakawa and Kiyomori, as he became the emperor's father-in-law. Until 1175, the two mightiest men in Japan remained cordial, but it was evident their relationship was corroding. Yet despite the resentment that slowly grew in Go-Shirakawa, he had to continue to rely on Kiyomori to subdue the ruffians, some of them being the armed Buddhist monks that ravaged the lands. But the might of the Taira clan grew too much, as Kiyomori was not only in the position of the old Fujiwara regents, but he also held considerable military might. So, Go-Shirakawa tried to politically outmaneuver him several times, which provoked Kiyomori to stage a coup in 1179. Go-Shirakawa was confined to his house, a large number of government officials were replaced, and Takakura was forced to abdicate in favor of his son from a Taira mother, Emperor Antoku. Yet the harshness of Kiyomori's rule, as well as his low-class origins, left him with little support. In the eastern provinces, Minamoto no Yoritomo and his clan challenged the Taira, starting the Genpei War which was to bring the insei system to an end and push Japan into the medieval era.

Before moving on to the war itself and the further developments in Japanese history, we should take a step back to look at the foreign relations of the late Heian period. As it was noted before, Japan was somewhat isolated from the start of this era, having only sporadic trade with Korea and to a lesser extent China. However, as political circumstances changed in Korea, Japanese traders weren't allowed to acquire goods from there, and so many of them turned to piracy, raiding Korean ports and ships. But thanks to the improvements in navigation, direct trade with China became easier, so in the second half of the 11th century, more direct relations started to open up. This increase is also connected with the rise of the Chinese Song dynasty and the rebirth of Chinese power. These relations also grew above simple trade as the Chinese emperor asked for the official Japanese envoy. Many traditionalists among the Japanese nobility were offended as this meant at least theoretical submission to the Chinese emperor. However, Kiyomori gladly accepted as the Taira clan was rather interested in connections with China, mainly because of trade. The resurgence of trade was important for the Japanese economy, as besides many other goods, it brought copper coins back into circulation across the empire. As domestic coins were out of circulation since the 10th century, this was rather stimulating for domestic trade as well as facilitating trade.

However, the renewed contact with the Chinese civilization wasn't enough to derail the unique socio-cultural development in Japan. In the two centuries prior to the Genpei War, the rising importance of the professional warriors, contrary to the earlier peasant conscripts, was irreversible. And they were tied to the traditional Japanese clan social structure as they were loyal to their local noble landholders. It is also vital to note that at this period these warriors weren't yet the knightly sword-wielding samurais. They were called bushi ("martial servitor") or saburai (earlier pronunciation of samurai), which were courtly titles of military attendants. They were chiefly horse riders who used bows as their primary weapons, resorting to swords and daggers only when they ran out of arrows. Two clans, Minamoto and Taira, both descendants of the imperial dynasty, managed to become leading warrior clans through fighting against the Emishi in the northeast, pirates and bandits across the lands, and suppressing local unrests and revolts. They were slowly bridging the gap between the courtly aristocrats in the capital and the lowly warriors in the provinces. But as their military might rose, so did their political influence. Soon they found themselves competing for supremacy over the entire state in the Genpei War, which as far as military might goes was solely a showdown between the Taira and Minamoto clans.

Painting of a battle from the Genpei War.
Source: https://commons.wikimedia.org

The war began when Go-Shirakawa's other son, feeling skipped over as a successor too many times, asked Minamoto no Yoritomo for help against Taira no Kiyomori. Despite the fact that the prince himself died within a few weeks of the beginning of the rebellion, the Minamoto clan continued the fight. Yoritomo used this as a justification to promote his own goals which were to create a system that bypassed the capital, granting the lands to his followers and making the eastern provinces basically his own vassals. He chose the city of Kamakura as his center because of its historical ties to his family. In the early stages of the war, conflicts were confined to the eastern provinces where the power of Minamoto laid, and it seemed Taira had the upper hand after winning several battles. However, the natural death of Kiyomori in 1181 weakened the Taira positions, and until 1183, both sides were primarily preoccupied with securing their positions in their own lands, avoiding large confrontations with each other. Then, in 1183, Yoritomo's cousin, Minamoto no Yoshinaka, managed to conquer Heian, which by that period became known as Kyoto ("capital city"). Taira fled to the west, taking Emperor Antoku with him. At this time, Yoshinaka tried to challenge Yoritomo for the role of the Minamoto leader while at the same time fighting the Taira.

Minamoto no Yoritomo (upper image) and Taira no Kiyomori (lower image) Source: https://commons.wikimedia.org

Yoritomo realized that attacking the capital would be futile if he didn't receive support. So, he contacted Go-Shirakawa who gave imperial sanction to his government, giving Yoritomo a lawful right to expand his fight across the entire empire as he was designated as its peacekeeper. That very same year, ex-emperor Go-Shirakawa ascended his grandson Go-Toba to the throne, negating Antoku's position with that move. By 1184, Yoshinaka was forced out of Kyoto and killed in a battle with Yoritomo's brother. Then, Minamoto forces, once again under the unquestioned leadership of Yoritomo, continued westward to deal with what remained of the Taira forces. But it wasn't an easy victory, as fighting continued for another year, culminating in the grand naval battle of Dan-no-ura, in the Shimonoseki Strait off the southern tip of Honshu. In that very battle, the Taira started with an upper hand despite being outnumbered, both because the tide was in their favor and because they were generally better sailors. Yet the tides changed when one of the Taira generals switched sides. Seeing that they were going to lose, many of the Taira started to commit suicide, with Kiyomori's widow taking her grandson, Emperor Antoku, with her to the depths of the sea. Within a month of that battle, the Genpei War ended with Yoritomo's victory.

The end result of the war was the end of the Heian period and the insei system. Some argue that it happened that very same year, as Yoritomo was granted the right to gather taxes. But more importantly, he gained permission from Go-Shirakawa to appoint military estate stewards (jitō) and military governors (shugo), who both basically became the main government officials in the provinces, giving the military class unprecedented political influence and power. And as his warriors were his retainers, it meant that Yoritomo became the de facto feudal overlord of Japan. Of course, this feudalization of Japan was a slow process as the majority of the land remained in the hands of its traditional owners for several more decades. Nonetheless, it marked a great turning point in Japanese society and history. Other historians argue that 1185 wasn't the final year of the insei, as Go-Shirakawa was still alive and blocking the final step in Yoritomo's plan. The two of them were locked in a political struggle for power which was only ended by the ex-emperor's death in 1192. That very same year, Yoritomo gained the old military title Sei-i Taishōgun ("Commander-in-Chief of the Expeditionary Force Against the Barbarians"), which was given to the leaders of expeditions against the Emishi. With this title, later abbreviated to the more familiar title of shōgun, Yoritomo became the most powerful man in Japan, starting the Kamakura period and Kamakura shōgunate (or Kamakura bakufu). Whatever exact year is chosen for the end of the insei and Heian period, it is clear that by the end of the 12th century, Japan entered its medieval era.

Until his death in 1199, Yoritomo was the unchallenged ruler and feudal dictator of Japan, especially after his victory over the Northern Fujiwara branch in 1189 and the expulsion of Go-Toba from the throne in 1198. But despite that, he never tried nor showed any intention of taking the imperial title for himself. The Yamato dynasty was still the religious epicenter of the country and the symbol of the empire. But thanks to the slow changes and precedents that date back from the Asuka period, by the time of the Kamakura shōgunate it became rather acceptable for the emperor to have pretty much no real authority, leaving state affairs to others. Nevertheless, Yoritomo's sons weren't as capable as he was. His father-in-law, Hōjō Tokimasa, who came from a branch of the Taira that sided with Minamoto in 1180, became the regent of his eldest son Yoriie. Yoritomo's son tried to push back against his regency, so Tokimasa stripped Yoriie of his shōgun title in 1203 and had him murdered within a year. His younger brother, Sanetomo, was more compliant, and so the Hōjō regency, through the title of shikken, became a permanent aspect of this early medieval period. And within a generation, the shōgun became a symbolic title without real authority, just like the emperor.

But the Hōjō regency wasn't unquestioned. In 1219, Sanetomo was assassinated, and the question of succession arose as he had no clear heir. This gave Hōjō Yoshitoki, Tokimasa's son, an excuse to strike harder against his opposition. But the more pressing matter for him was the question of the next shōgun. He wanted someone from the imperial family but was denied by Go-Toba, who was gathering support for himself in Kyoto as he was trying to capitalize on the unrest of the warriors beneath the ruling classes and the affairs that were shaking the political scene in Kamakura. Go-Toba refused, using his imperial right of choosing and appointing high-ranking officials in the government, which in essence is what a shōgun was. Instead, he chose an infant Fujiwara to be the next shōgun. But then he changed his mind, refusing to install a new shōgun altogether, probably thinking that the Hōjō and the entire Kamakura shogunate was weak enough for him to restore the imperial authority. By mid-1221, Go-Toba declared war on the Hōjō, but his army, filled with soldiers all over Japan, was an incoherent and unorganized group that stood practically no chance against the well-trained warriors from the eastern provinces which fought for the shōgunate. Go-Toba and his party were exiled, and all traces of imperial authority was destroyed, leaving control over the state in the hands of the Hōjō regents.

Emperor Go-Toba. Source: https://commons.wikimedia.org

The system that was created was of dual polities, one in Kamakura, which was headed by the Hōjō designated shōguns, first from the Fujiwara clan and then from imperial princes. The other was based in Kyoto around the imperial dynasty and the court. With the expansion of the shugo and jitō, the power of the bakufu was expanding, bolstered with the military force at its disposal. Hōjō regents also acquired legislative and judicial powers for the shōgunate, or to be more precise, for themselves. Yoshitoki's son Yasutoki became the new shikken in 1224 and further reorganized the bakufu. He created a board of councilors as a governmental organ of the shogunate and then went on to promulgate the Goseibai Shikimoku, the code of law for the bakufu in 1232 which stipulated how vassal relations of the shugo and jitō should function. Yet despite the fact that his regency is seen as the golden age of Hōjō supremacy, his position wasn't completely unquestionable. Although the emperor's position was more symbolic at this point, he still presided, at least nominally, over a Chinese-style administration that covered the civil population in provinces that were still officially under imperial control. And from these, he received taxes, which given the right circumstances were enough to seriously challenge the Kamakura shōgunate.

Yasutoki's life ended in 1242, once again putting the delicate political balance at risk. That year the bakufu forced a change of emperors, enthroning Go-Saga, a man who wasn't a favorite of the courtiers in Kyoto. Yasutoki's grandson Tsunetoki became the new shikken and tried to reaffirm his position in 1244 by forcing the current shōgun Fujiwara no Yoritsune to abdicate in favor of his underage son Yoritsugu. In 1246, Tsunetoki died, being succeeded by his brother Tokiyori. That very same year Emperor Go-Saga was elevated to the position of ex-emperor, and with his help, Kamakura pushed Kyoto to update its bureaucracy according to its own scheme. The quick succession in both capitals caused several political intrigues, but the Hōjō clan remained firmly in control. Tokiyori even went a step further to stabilize his own reign. In 1252, he instated an imperial prince, Munetaka, the son of Go-Saga, as a shōgun. Thus, he had puppets in both capitals, which were coincidentally father and son. This managed to prolong the stability of the Hōjō regime, but in 1263, Tokiyori died, and certain instabilities started to manifest themselves. Most notable was the quarrel inside the Hōjō clan itself, as certain branches tried to challenge the main line.

This led to some minor administrative changes in the bakufu, but it was the foreign threat of the Kublai Khan's Mongol empire which reached Korean shores that managed to put aside all political turbulence among the Japanese. In 1286, Kublai sent a letter to the "king of Japan" through his Korean vassals, the kingdom of Koryŏ which in previous centuries united the peninsula and had some connections with Japan. Through a letter, the Mongol ruler ominously demanded a tribute and recognition of his supremacy. It seems that his ultimate goal was gathering prestige for his dynasty, not actual conquest. But both Kamakura and Kyoto decided to ignore this request. The shōgunate started to prepare defenses, realizing that the Mongol threat was both real and serious. With a sword hanging over their heads, the Japanese found national unity, and all internal struggles for power were ceased for the moment. Yet Kublai Khan was persistent in trying to solve this diplomatically, sending several more envoys asking for simple tribute and recognition, all returning empty-handed. By 1271, the imperial court received a final ultimatum from the Khan and once again did not respond to the request. The bakufu ordered that defenses in Kyushu should be prepared, with all soldiers from that region returning to their estates and by pacifying all outlaws through military actions.

With the imminent threat of invasion, the main Hōjō branch eliminated all their opponents in the bakufu in 1272 as they wanted to have a secure situation in the homeland. Sources tell us that the atmosphere in Japan was full of worry and tension, yet the invasion didn't come until 1274 as Kublai Khan decided to finish conquering the southern Chinese territories first. The Mongols then sent 15,000 of their own soldiers accompanied by 8,000 Korean warriors in about 800 ships. When they arrived, the invaders had more success than the defenders. They were better equipped, had superior commanders, and were used to group movement and fighting. In contrast to that, Japanese warriors, having no major conflicts since 1221, lacked capable commanders and were used to one-on-one fights, even in major battles. Slowly, the Mongol troops progressed. But those victories were only minor ones, and the Mongols were unable to establish a good bridgehead to continue their invasion. At the same time, they were slowly running out of supplies as they were constantly returning to their ships, unable to gather provisions from the occupied land. So, after several weeks, the Mongol army withdrew, losing about 200 ships in a storm. Nonetheless, this Japanese victory didn't eliminate the foreign threat.

A painting of a battle between Japanese and Mongol armies.
Source: https://commons.wikimedia.org

Hōjō Tokimune, who was shikken since 1268, realized that further strengthening of Japan's defenses was needed. He ordered that both military and civil leaders, i.e., owners of jitō and shōen, to contribute to building fortifications and walls on the coastline. He further conscripted all warriors, without regard to whom they were subjugated to. In 1275, Tokimune organized warriors in the Kyushu region into combined units of two to three provinces. Each unit would serve actively three months per year, while in the event of a crisis all of them would be mobilized. This became a heavy burden for the warriors of Kyushu, but the shikken also demanded that the nobles live frugally so that they wouldn't burden the population more than needed. Finally, he replaced military governors in strategically important provinces with trusted members of the Hōjō clan. So, in 1281 when Kublai Khan sent his second invasion, Japan was ready, or at least more prepared than the last time. But now Kublai was determined to conquer Japan, especially as the Japanese had executed all the envoys he sent since 1274. For this invasion, he amassed 2 armies carried by 2 fleets, one from Korea and the other from southern China. Together they had 4,400 ships and about 140,000 men, an army comparable in size with the Allied forces attacking Normandy during World War II.

Later painting of the "divine wind."
Source: https://commons.wikimedia.org

However, the Mongol army, consisting of Chinese and Korean soldiers as well, who attacked from two sides lacked motivation and coordination between them. Their ships were also gathered and built hastily, many of them not suitable for an open ocean. And they were met by fortified shores and prepared Japanese defenders. So, the invaders weren't able to create a bridgehead, withdrawing after fierce resistance. Finally, the two Mongol fleets merged and planned the final attack. While some of the attacking forces were on the coast, a devastating typhoon destroyed the majority of the Mongol fleet, forcing their generals to retreat and leave the remaining troops to be slaughtered by the Japanese. According to the sources, between 70 and 90% of the invading army was destroyed. So, in the end, it was both preparation, determination, and pure luck that saved Japan from being conquered. Of course, the deeply religious Japanese of that era saw it as a godly intervention. To Shinto and Buddhist priests it was a "divine wind," or kamikaze in Japanese, that saved their country by a typhoon, claiming this was proof that their country was chosen by the gods. This idea remained implanted in the collective consciousness of the Japanese until the end of World War II, where it manifested through the suicide pilots who took the name of kamikaze, protecting their land from the air.

This national unity combined with the tightened rule of the Hōjō regency was achieved by the Mongol threat. But with the enemy defeated, this pressure was alleviated. With the death of Kublai Khan in 1294, Japan ceased to be in any danger. But the bakufu leaders didn't want to relax their control, asking warriors to remain alert without giving them proper compensation. Tension rose among them, blaming the Kamakura shōgunate for their misfortune. And as years passed, the Hōjō leaders became less competent to command and punish the insubordinate warriors who then turned to fight among themselves. Issues of outlaws and pirates also plagued the rising economy of medieval Japan. While that weakened the military positions of the Kamakura court, affairs in Kyoto destabilized its political power. There since the 1270s, bakufu leaders practiced switching the line of succession between two branches of the Yamato dynasty. This caused too much bad blood between them. Despite trying to debilitate the imperial power by this move, emperors of the late 13th and early 14th centuries started to show less compliance to the shōgunate. Some of them even reformed their courts and tax gatherings to improve their own position and resources. This culminated with the ascension of Emperor Go-Daigo to the throne in 1318.

He was a capable ruler who through a stroke of luck managed to rule without previous emperors meddling in his affairs, as most of them were either dead or out of the political life. In such a position, he started dreaming about restoring the imperial authority from the "golden age" of Emperor Daigo, his namesake, from the early Heian period. Attempting to exploit the weaknesses of the bakufu, which were becoming more and more evident, in 1324 he planned his first rebellion, but the anti-bakufu movement was discovered, and Go-Daigo barely managed to talk his way out of banishment. He laid low for some time before arranging another conspiracy to throw over the shōgunate in 1331. The movement was once again discovered, but this time after losing his generals, Go-Daigo stepped forward as the leader of the anti-bakufu forces. This widened the support for the movement, but the bakufu forces won, and he was removed from the throne and exiled. However, this didn't eradicate all of the anti-shōgunate elements. Gathered around his son, the anti-bakufu, now filled with outlaws and warriors without feudal lords, started to cause trouble around Kyoto. This was when the Hōjō made their biggest and probably fatal mistake. In 1333, they sent Ashikaga Takauji to deal with the ensuing unrest, but he harbored antipathy toward the Hōjō and kept in touch with the exiled Go-Daigo.

Takauji, who belonged to a branch of the Minamoto clan, realized that his forces combined with the army behind the rebel forces were enough to topple the current regime. Thanks to his contempt of the Hōjō clan, he easily switched sides. Go-Daigo came back from exile, and together they marched on Kamakura. Sensing the imminent fall, another member of the Minamoto clan, Nitta Yoshisada, rebelled in the east, attacking the bakufu capital and destroying the forces of the shōgunate. The majority of the Hōjō that survived the fighting committed suicide. Go-Daigo seized the throne from the bakufu-installed Emperor Kōgon, and thus, the first Japanese shōgunate fell. With the fall of Kamakura, the early medieval period of Japanese history ended, leaving a formed feudal system and ideals to shape its future development.

Chapter 5 – Late Medieval Japan

In the early medieval period of Japanese history, feudalism and a militaristic society were developed, transforming the Land of the Rising Sun into the civilization we know today. It was a unified country with an emperor as a purely symbolic religious ruler, and it was divided between martial aristocratic clans which fought amongst themselves for supremacy and the title of shōgun. It was also a deeply religious country with an intermixing of two faiths. One was Buddhism which branched out into several different teachings and cults, and the other was Shintoism, the original Japanese religion which celebrated the imperial dynasty as well as millions of gods. But during this period, there was still a resonance of the classical Japanese society there as well. For one, the emperor still had an echo of the imperial political authority that emperors in the past held, while the supposedly all-mighty shōgun was overpowered by his regents like the old emperors were. Those remnants of the bygone era were to be lost in the late medieval period.

But before that final transformation was to happen, there was a rather short period in which Emperor Go-Daigo tried to revive the past. In what is today called the Kenmu Restoration, he tried to recreate the old statutory system in which civil nobles held all important governmental positions, answering only to the emperor, while soldiers were nothing more than just servants. He started rearranging his government, confiscating jitō estates and giving them as shōen to his noble followers. With this reckless dealing with land issues, he neglected to take care of the commoners, thus alienating them as well. But most importantly, Go-Daigo ignored Ashikaga Takauji's wish for the shōgun title. Instead, he gave it to his son in an attempt to control both Kyoto and Kamakura. This was the final straw for Takauji, and the former allies clashed. The emperor sent Nitta Yoshisada to fight against him, but he lost, as Takauji had more followers from the warrior class since they saw him fighting for their cause. By 1336, Go-Daigo was routed from Kyoto, ending his restoration and enthroning Kōmyō as the new emperor. In turn, he gave the shōgun title to Takauji, which marked a beginning of the Ashikaga shōgunate (Ashikaga bakufu) or, as it was also known, the Muromachi shogunate, named after a district in Kyoto where later shōguns based their headquarters.

Despite that, the enemies of the new bakufu weren't stepping down. Go-Daigo retreated to the mountains of Yoshino in the Nara Province, south of Kyoto. There, in early 1337, he set up the Southern Court that opposed the Northern Court which was under the patronage of the bakufu and still resided in Kyoto. For the first and only time, the imperial dynasty split into two branches that claimed to reign at the same time. Japan entered an era of never-ending civil war, as fighting between the two sides continued. For most of this fighting, the Ashikaga shōgunate had the upper hand, but for a brief period in the early 1350s, the Southern Court managed to turn the tides. Because of internal division, Ashikaga Tadayoshi, Takauji's brother switched sides and managed to take both Kamakura, which was still the capital of the bakufu, and Kyoto. Yet Takauji managed to beat him twice, restoring the supremacy of the Northern Court. He and his brother reconciled, but Ashikaga died rather quickly after this, presumably poisoned by Takauji. Left without a serious army and a capable general, the Southern Court returned to guerilla warfare and small skirmishes through which they continued the civil war.

Ashikaga period samurais. Source: https://commons.wikimedia.org

The long reign of Ashikaga Takauji ended in 1358 when he died, leaving the title of shōgun to his grandson Yoshiakira. Losing such a capable leader was a huge setback for the Ashikaga bakufu, and the Southern Court forces once again posed a more serious threat. But the shōgunate was strong enough to endure, and in 1368, he was succeeded by his son Ashikaga Yoshimitsu, who proved to be a more talented leader and politician. He realized that mere military might would never bring stability to the Ashikaga rule, so he sought to gain legitimacy by gaining civil offices in the imperial government. Despite not gaining any actual authority through them, he received much-needed political backing. It was him who moved the center of the bakufu from Kamakura to the Muromachi district in Kyoto in 1378 and during the 1380s continued to climb up the ranks of imperial officials. Yoshimitsu's biggest success came in 1392 when he managed to persuade the Southern Court to reconcile with the Northern branch of the imperial dynasty. He promised them that two family lines would switch on the throne, a promise which he then ignored, leading to the extinction of the Southern branch. Two years later, he was awarded the title of Grand Chancellor of State, the highest-ranking position in the civil government. Thus, he undisputedly became the most influential person of his era.

This merger of political and military power in the hands of the shōgun wasn't limited to ranks and titles. Yoshimitsu also integrated the bureaucracies of both governments, turning more and more civil prerogatives to the military governors, or shugo. For example, they were given the right to gather taxes. And in turn, members of the military aristocracy following his example started gathering ranks and titles appropriate to civil leaders, for example, the position of provincial governor. Furthermore, with rising questions of land disputes, more and more aristocrats started to group their estates in one place, making it easier to control and defend, while at the same time leaving the bulk of their inheritance to a single successor. This prevented splitting their family lands into smaller pieces. And indeed, those shugos who managed to gather great estates for themselves were the ones who benefited the most from the new regime, slowly turning into what modern historians call shugo-daimyō, meaning they were half military governors of the Kamakura and quasi-independent regional lords of the 14th century. While Yoshimitsu was still alive, he was still able to control them, but soon after his death in 1408, they started to ignore the edicts and orders of the Ashikaga shōguns.

Before his death, Yoshimitsu set two important precedents. Firstly, he abdicated in favor of his son, creating the title ex-shōgun, and as all authority remained in his hands, it was strikingly similar to the insei system of the late Heian period. Secondly, he reopened both trade and diplomatic relations with China, which was at the time ruled by the famous Ming dynasty. This revived the trade economy of Japan, allowing for an influx of coins, silk, and medicines, as well as Chinese culture in general through books, paintings, and similar products. More importantly, Yoshimitsu accepted the Chinese recognition of him as the "king of Japan." His gains were twofold; he gained wider Asian recognition both for himself and for Japan, and he was the primary benefiter of trade as it was taxed by the bakufu officials. This set up the precedent that the emperor shouldn't bother with foreign relations and instead leave those all up to the shōgun's will. Of course, many saw this as a usurpation of imperial prerogatives, but Yoshimitsu defended himself by explaining that he was merely shielding the emperor from facing the actuality of a letter of investiture and its disgrace. Some sources do mention that he was indeed planning to usurp the position of the Japanese monarch, but he died before actually trying anything, so historians aren't sure if those were really his intentions.

Whatever Yoshimitsu's actual plans were, after his death, the Muromachi bakufu was without a proper successor. As the central authority of the Ashikaga regime was wavering, the power of the local warlords was rising. Paired with that was the growing importance of Zen Buddhism, which first started spreading in the late 12th and early 13th centuries. It was brought from China, and its ideals were the perfect fit for the increasingly militaristic society of Japan. By the early 15th century, it became the most important religious faction as most samurais and shugo were following its word. Its teachings of simplicity, restraint, and discipline were the perfect ideals for a soldier, but it also preached confronting death without fear. These principles also spread into the Japanese culture, where they were displayed through the ideals of subdued taste, naturalism, elegant simplicity, and tranquil otherworldliness. Remnants of those ideas are still seen in modern Japanese culture. All of this made the Japanese society of the 15th and 16th century strikingly militaristic, and the bakufu was losing its capabilities to control the feudal lords. In 1441, the current shōgun was assassinated for trying to regain some of the lost authority, as local rebellions and skirmishes between the shugo became ever more common.

The state of things led to a full-out civil war in the 1460s. It erupted mainly because of the succession issues of the Ashikaga shōguns. Yoshimasa, shōgun at the time, was childless, so he adopted his own brother as his successor but surprisingly had a son in 1464. This drove a wedge between the brothers and the feudal lords that supported them. This hostility blew up in an open war known as the Ōnin War in 1467. It was fought throughout Japan, but the toughest fighting was around Kyoto. After a decade of bloody battles, the war subsided without a real victor, despite the fact that Yoshimasa was succeeded by his son Yoshihisa in 1473. The real result of the war was a disintegration of the bakufu's control over the feudal lords. They stayed nominal leaders of both the military and civil governments, but the warlords were now starting to deal with each other in their own struggle for power. And so, the period from 1467 to 1603 became known as the Sengoku period (Sengoku Jidai), or Age of the Warring States. From that point onward, the transformation of the military aristocracy from shugo to daimyō, a great feudal lord, was complete, as they were now pretty much independent and embroiled in almost never-ending warring among themselves with only nominal regard and respect for both the emperor and the shōgun.

A battle from the Ōnin War. Source: https://commons.wikimedia.org

Rather quickly, old clans and aristocratic families were displaced by capable leaders from smaller families, who rose to success through their cold-bloodedness and calculations. Most of these were former subordinates of the nobles who remained on their estates while their superiors were chasing after influence in the capital. Chaos ensued, everyone was fighting against everyone, fragile alliances would change quickly, and all sense of national unity was lost. Battles and armies grew larger, with up to 50,000 on one side. No longer were samurai the only soldiers on the field. However, they remained the superior force. Trained, mounted, and better equipped, they were rather similar to the medieval European knights. But the bulk of the fighting force was common foot soldiers known as ashigaru. They were supplied by their commanders and served under the military command of the samurai. And as they all fought as organized armies, battles were no longer fought one-on-one. During these bloody times, both the emperor and the shōgun were unable to gather enough authority to keep the feudal lords in line, but the governmental mechanisms of both the bakufu and the imperial administration survived, serving as the legal framework for the civil war.

By the mid-16th century, the war became a matter of everyday business. Despite that, the economy was growing. Many of the lords promoted economic expansion and trade as the size of their armies depended on the depth of their treasuries. This led to the cultivation of new lands, advances in agricultural techniques, and growth of the trade market. And as the most needed items were swords and armor, rudimentary forms of metalworking industries also developed. They were helped by foreign trade with China and Korea, where those items were exported alongside copper and sulfur. More importantly, in the 1540s, the first contacts with the Europeans, or to be more exact with the Portuguese, were made. Besides bringing Christianity, which never took much hold in Japan, they brought firearms which radically changed the nature of warfare. The feudal lords who were quick enough to adapt and adopt the new weapons started to gain the upper hand against their more traditional opponents. One such person was Oda Nobunaga, a daimyō from the Owari Province (part of the present-day Aichi Prefecture). As a perceptive strategist, he arose from a somewhat minor status to substantial power through a number of victories over rival lords. Because of that, in the 1560s, he got involved with the succession dispute of the bakufu on the request of the claimant Ashikaga Yoshiaki.

Being a very talented general, Nobunaga managed to capture Kyoto and install Yoshiaki as the new, and as it was going to turn out last, Ashikaga shōgun. But by that point, Nobunaga had become the most powerful daimyo, and he started to rule using Yoshiaki as a mere puppet. The new shōgun disliked that and used what was left of his influence and power to gain support against his former ally. This resulted in Yoshiaki's banishment from Kyoto in 1573, ending the Ashikaga shōgunate even though Yoshiaki retained his title until he officially resigned in 1588. In an attempt to tighten his hold over the country, Nobunaga started waging wars against other feudal lords, some being his former allies. At the same time, he also openly attacked Buddhist temples, which during the civil war grew their influence and power through their warrior monks. In these wars and attacks, he showed no mercy, killing captives and massacring the civil population if they got in his way. In 1575, it was Nobunaga who first used a substantial number of muskets to win a battle, the Battle of Nagashino, showing his ability to recognize the potential of the firearms that the Europeans brought to Japan. And by 1580, it seemed that Nobunaga was about to unify Japan once again as no other feudal lord was able to match his power. Yet his mission to reunite the Land of the Rising Sun was cut short in 1582 when one of his generals turned against him for unknown reasons. He caught Nobunaga unprepared, attacking him when he was traveling without guards. In his last defiant act, Nobunaga killed himself rather than having his head fall in the hands of his enemies.

European ships docked in a Japanese harbor.
Source: https://commons.wikimedia.org

It was no coincidence that two other daimyōs that went to fulfill his plans were his own vassals. The first to step forth to the stage was Toyotomi Hideyoshi. He was also an accomplished general and tactician who saw his opportunity in the death of his suzerain. He caught and punished the traitor, depicting himself as the protector of the Oda clan, and then used his gained power and influence to install Nobunaga's infant grandson as the head of the family. This made Hideyoshi the next leading daimyō in Japan. Another great lord that served under Nobunaga was Tokugawa Ieyasu, who slowly gained lands and power through his service to Nobunaga. As he was Hideyoshi's main rival at that point, they clashed in a struggle for power in 1584, but the campaign proved to be indecisive. Instead of pursuing the matter to the end, Ieyasu stepped down and accepted Hideyoshi as his superior. This allowed Hideyoshi to continue Nobunaga's dream of unification as he took down any other competitors one by one, often helped by Ieyasu. The last one to fall was the Go-Hōjō clan, unrelated to the previous Hōjō family, which fell in 1590. With this, Japan was unified, though only for a short time.

Both Nobunaga and Hideyoshi didn't become the shōgun, but the latter did take other courtly titles such as regent to legitimize his own rule. He treated Japan like his own domain, disregarding the traditional bureaucratic apparatus. And it proved to be a quite effective way to rule. He quickly gained a lot of power and wealth and then proceeded to invade Korea in 1592 and 1597. His goal was to conquer not only Korea but China as well. Despite some military victories and short-term territorial gains, both campaigns were total failures. This is why some historians believe that since he was a competent general, he would have known those attacks would be futile and that conquest wasn't his ultimate goal. Instead, they think he sent unreliable samurais and generals to die, but this interpretation remains questionable. Regardless, his hold over Japan was secured in the 1590s, but his legacy wasn't. He had an infant son, and to protect Toyotomi supremacy, Hideyoshi formed the Council of Five Elders (Go-Tairō) consisting of the five greatest feudal lords of the time to act as regents to his son when he died. Among them was Tokugawa Ieyasu, who after the fall of Go-Hōjō was given their territories in exchange for his. Hideyoshi did this to weaken his rather questionable ally, moving him farther away from the capital and forcing him to use time and resources in establishing his power base in the new domain.

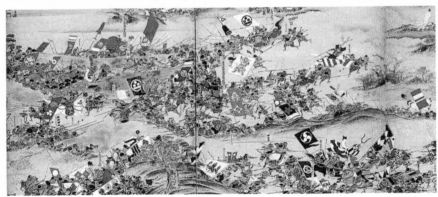

The Battle of Sekigahara. Source: https://commons.wikimedia.org

However, instead of weakening him, this only strengthened him as he was awarded more land than he previously held which proved to be a great source of income and strength. There, Ieyasu chose the small fishing village of Edo as his new capital because of its central position in his newly gained territory. Under his rule, as well as of his successors, that little village grew into a true metropolis we today know as Tokyo. So, in 1598 when Hideyoshi died, Ieyasu was the most powerful daimyō, and for a year, he was kept in check by the other council members. Then one of the more experienced regents died, and Tokugawa Ieyasu saw his opportunity. Japan was once again in a civil war now divided between pro-Toyotomi and pro-Tokugawa factions. The sheer military power of Ieyasu attracted some former Toyotomi generals, while through his political capabilities, he managed to attract two of the other council members. The two groups clashed in the Battle of Sekigahara, located midway between Nagoya and Kyoto, and the Tokugawa forces emerged victorious. Afterward, no one could question his position as the leader of Japan. Ieyasu legitimized it by acquiring the position of shōgun in 1603, finally uniting Japan under one rule.

Thus, Oda Nobunaga, Toyotomi Hideyoshi, and Tokugawa Ieyasu were to become known as the three unifiers of Japan, military leaders who in succession took command over the lands and finally brought the Warring States period to an end. The differences in their characters are best represented with a famous Japanese saying which has those three leaders stumbling upon a songbird that refused to sing. Trying to resolve the matter, Nobunaga said, "I'll kill it if it doesn't sing." "I'll persuade it to sing," Hideyoshi replied. Ieyasu added, "I'll wait until it sings." These answers represent what was needed for unification to be accomplished—impulsiveness, self-confidence, and patience. With a combination of those, in 1603 Japan got its new shōgun family and peace, and it is when the Edo era and Tokugawa shōgunate started, pulling Japan out of the medieval times and into the modern age.

Chapter 6 – Japanese Society

Japanese society as it evolved through the centuries became ever more complex, more so than most other civilizations throughout history. This complexity comes from the fact that in this civilization the class hierarchy was sometimes parallel, like when it comes to the position of the warriors and nobles. It was also constantly changing through time, with huge local variations in medieval times as the country lacked true centralization. Another complicating factor was the familiar clan divisions. But in this chapter, an outline will be given of their society, with the most focus given to the feudalized and decentralized society of medieval Japan.

Japanese imperial banner. Source: https://commons.wikimedia.org

From the beginning of Japanese history, or at least the history of the Yamato, on top of all the people stood the monarch from the Yamato dynasty, a tradition continued even today. In the beginning, they were kings, but by the 8th century, they adopted the imperial title becoming heavenly sovereigns or tennō. In the early days, these monarchs were the true rulers of the country, with unquestionable authority, political influence, and even military might. It is through a combination of those that they managed to unite small kingdoms on the isles and actually create Japan. But as we have seen in previous chapters, their role over time became increasingly symbolic, with rare outbursts of some capable emperors who tried to recreate direct imperial rule. Nonetheless, no matter how symbolic their presence became, no warlord or noble dared to think about replacing the Yamato dynasty on the throne due to their religious role. As adopted from Chinese ideals, it was the ruler who was tasked with appeasing the gods for the good of the entire country. On top of that, they were mythologically connected to the gods that created Japan, and in their eyes, overthrowing the imperial dynasty would cause Japan to lose its divine protection. This long tradition is why even today, after 125 monarchs, Japan is officially ruled by the emperor in the constitutional parliamentary monarchy, despite not having any sovereignty.

In the ancient and classical times, it was the nobles who were the highest class beneath the emperor. They filled all the important positions in the government, actually helping the emperor rule the country. They were rich, educated, and owned large estates that funded their lifestyle. Despite sometimes leading armies, they weren't that connected to warfare, as in those eras war wasn't as common. Their power lay in the political influence they gained in the court. Through marriages, intrigues, and affairs, some of the nobles managed to become more powerful than even the emperors, usually seen in the position of regent some of them held. But as times changed and reliance on simple military strength became more important than political maneuvering, their importance dwindled. Their estates were absorbed by the warlords, the court lost its authority, and like the emperor, their position became more symbolic than actually relevant. Despite that, they were still held in high esteem because of their noble heritage, education, and inclination toward arts, with some of them managing to find a way to interfere with politics even in the medieval warrior dominated society.

Ashikaga Takauji, founder of the Ashikaga shōgunate.
Source: https://commons.wikimedia.org

From the 11ᵗʰ century onwards, society in Japan became increasingly militaristic as the importance of the warrior class rose. The first to gain influence was actually nobles who turned to war as their main focus for livelihood. It was these warriors with aristocratic descent who were able to combine their military strength and political influence to become either shōguns or shikkens, concentrating governmental authority in their hands and ruling instead of, or more precisely in the name of, the emperor. It was they who replaced the noble regents of the Heian period who were in control of the country. As such, they were at the top of the warrior class hierarchy. Below them were the so-called gokenin or shōgunal vassals. For their support, they received large estates and served in the bureaucracy of the bakufu, most often as estate stewards (jitō) and military governors (shugo). There was a relatively small number of gokenin, maybe up to 2,000 of them, but as they themselves had vassals and retainers, they were rather powerful and wealthy. And through this cascading feudal system, they brought a large number of soldiers into control of the shōgunate. In the late medieval period, during the civil war, it is from their ranks that the semi-autonomous feudal lords, or daimyo, arose. It is also worth noting that these high-ranking warriors were also usually well educated, as they also had to serve in the shōgunal administration.

Below the gokenin class were the samurai. Despite our present-day view on them as knightly warriors, it was actually a soldier class. They were mid-ranked in the social hierarchy and much more numerous than the gokenin. Samurai warriors also owned estates, though much smaller than the gokenin, had a decent income, and some of them were also educated. But their main focus was on fighting skills, and they were indeed the elite fighters in medieval Japan, serving primarily as cavalry. And though some of them were from noble descent, this wasn't a prerequisite to becoming a samurai. Similar to the gokenin, they also had their own vassals who were common foot soldiers. These were commoner warriors that served as the bulk of the fighting force. They were trained in combat but lacked all other education, had only small parcels needed to support their families, and were rather dependent on the other two warrior classes. Both them and the samurai spent most of their time on their own lands tending to them, unlike the gokenin who were often busy with developments in the capital and the government. And despite the idealized picture of Japanese warriors being loyal to a fault, during the 15th- and 16th-century civil wars, their allegiance was always questionable. Other aspects of Japanese warfare and soldiers will be discussed in another chapter.

Continuing down on the social hierarchy came farmers and peasants, known collectively as hyakushō. As the lower classes of Japanese society, they represented the tax base of the country, usually paying the land tax for the fields they were working on. There was also a class distinction between the farmers. Those who were wealthier and owned their own lands were called myoshu. They were local landholders who were rather independent, and they sometimes served for the estate (shoen) proprietors. Below them were kenin which literally translated means inferior people. They worked the land of the domain officials, estate owners, or in some cases even for myōshu farmers. Kenin had no rights to independently manage the lands they worked on nor freedom of movement. As they could be bought or sold and were usually linked to the land they worked on since they were a part of the estate inheritance, they are rather similar to the position of European feudal serfs. In the late medieval period, their social status started to change as kenin gained land rights as tenant farmers. Occasionally, some of the farmers had the opportunity to become warrior-farmers if their lords needed to fill up their armies. Warrior-farmers that showed enough skill and aptitude in fighting could then become part of the warrior class and work his way up the social hierarchy. Despite the fact that the living conditions and social freedoms of farmer sounds rather hard or unfair, it varied across Japan. It depended on local traditions and relations between the landowners and the farmers. In some cases, even kenin were treated as part of the extended family that controlled or owned the land.

At the bottom of the social hierarchy were the social outcasts. One group of them were called eta, or hereditary outcasts. These were members of families that worked on tasks that were seen as religiously impure, usually connected with working with the disposal or treatment of animals and animal hides, like butchers and tanners. Another group of social outcasts was hinin. Their position was a result of a social transgression, usually committing a crime. But one could also become hinin if their occupations were deemed socially improper, such as acting and other entertainment professions. Slaves, or nuhi, were also part of the lowest groups of

Japanese society, but the information on them is actually rather questionable, in some aspects strikingly similar to kenin, and they never represented any significant percentage of the population. What is known is that by the end of the 16th century, elites regarded slavery as outdated and morally wrong, and in 1590, Toyotomi Hideyoshi officially banned slavery, though some forms of "forced labor" persisted through the next centuries.

So far, all of the social classes can be easily pinpointed in the hierarchy. But artisans' and merchants' positions in their society is rather hard to define. When we look at the theoretical division of the Japanese social order, it is clear that craftsmen and traders were at the bottom, just above the outcasts. This shouldn't be so surprising as this order was created in classical Japan when both of these economical fields were rather undeveloped. But as the medieval era was coming to an end, these two classes blossomed. Artisans became highly appreciated and sought-after as they were able to create objects that were either needed, like high-quality swords and muskets, or desired, like fine quality silk. On the other hand, traders were able to earn a lot of money, becoming rather influential in society, even though they were sometimes looked down upon. It is important to note that these classes rose in stature with the development of the entire Japanese economy in the late medieval period and were linked with the increased financial capabilities of the feudal lords who wanted to satisfy their desires through acquiring precious goods. And as artisans and merchants became more important, they started to gather in guilds (za) to create monopolies over the goods they made or sold.

The emergence of these two classes is indicative that the Japanese economy was booming from the Heian period onwards. The roots of this expansion were laid in agriculture. Technological advances such as the development of double cropping and the use of iron tools managed to increase farming production and created surplus that kickstarted local trade. Commerce proved to be a good source of income, and it was so desired by the feudal lords and nobles that they did their best to promote it. Gradually, merchants traveled across all of Japan, linking the entire country into one commercial network. This allowed the development of highly-skilled artisans who could create valuable items which weren't suitable for everyday use and everyone's pockets. With more items to offer and more money to buy, Japanese elites slowly started venturing into international trade, which prior to the late medieval times was sporadic and limited in scope. First, they connected with Korea, then with China, which was Japan's most important trading partner, and finally in the 16th century came the Europeans. This trade further developed the Japanese economy, allowing for an influx of copper coins which slowly started to replace the barter system. Gold and silver coins were also used but were more limited, as most of the population wasn't wealthy enough for it. This also shows that there were large financial differences in Japanese society, and only merchants and certain members of the elites were actually living comfortably. Farmers, artisans, and lower-class warriors remained poor, sometimes even resorting to social protests and revolts in an attempt to better their positions and livelihoods.

However, Japanese society was too rigid and hierarchal for these revolts to achieve any substantial gains. That rigidness can also be seen in the position of women in society. In the classical era, women were treated more equally. The best example of this was the fact that in those times there were several female monarchs that actually ruled Japan, be it with the title of a queen or an empress. That being said, they weren't really equal to men as they still held all the important offices and were generally in charge of the country, estate, and the family. Yet the arrival of Buddhism and Chinese thought, which was much more patriarchal than the Japanese culture, brought down the position of women. Some Buddhist schools saw women as impure because of menstruation and childbirth, and this reflected on their position in society. They were banned from inheriting estates and were in a way subordinate to their fathers and husbands. And as Japan was continually fractioned, women were often used to reinforce alliances through marriages or as hostages, making them merely a political chip. On the other hand, wives of warriors were in some cases trained in combat, and were not only able but expected to defend their home and domain while men were at war. And Buddhist temples did provide sanctuary to women who were trying to escape abusive marriages. It's noteworthy to point out that these examples were limited to women of higher status, so the image of the actual position of women in ancient Japanese society is still obscured by the lack of information.

An Asuka period mural depicting women.
Source: https://commons.wikimedia.org

Finally, the last quintessential part of the Japanese social structure were clans, which gave horizontal depth to an already quite vertically structured society. This division on kinships began in a time when the Yamato dynasty ruled over only their own kingdom, and though at one point the central government tried to suppress clans, they remained too important to be dissolved. With that being said, clans were only a part of the elite circles. Commoners usually remained limited to only their immediate relatives as they simply weren't rich enough to establish such a complex social structure. To aristocrats, clans were one of the most important parts of life. First of all, not all clans were equal. Some were large and influential, like the Fujiwara or Minamoto, while others remained smaller, though still respectable. And some clans were specialized for certain tasks, like warfare or administration. Despite the mutual respect the clans had among themselves, they were almost constantly in conflict with one another, fighting for supremacy. In a society like this, loyalty to one's clan was supreme, in some cases coming before the loyalty to the country or the emperor. Clans also played an important role in religious life as well, as most of them had their own temples and ancestor cults. And on top of the clan hierarchy was the head of the family, who commanded all other members of the clan as he wished. It was also possible to adopt someone into the clan, which was usually either to bolster the clan's strength or as a token of appreciation for someone's service.

Loyalty was truly appreciated in medieval Japanese society, which was quite divided and distinctly hierarchical. It both reflected the development of Japanese culture and history while at the same time affecting them as well. Even today, remnants of these divisions and traditions are seen in the Japanese civilization. The highly structured and hierarchical system is most obvious in modern-day corporate life in Japan where just through greetings and bowing you can see who is who's superior.

Chapter 7 – Warriors of Ancient Japan

As Japanese culture and society became militaristic in its nature, warriors became one of the most important parts of this civilization. So, without understanding them, one cannot understand Japan and its history. This is especially important because modern misconceptions presented through movies and books strongly influence our vision of medieval Japanese soldiers. The simplest example of this is that one often thinks of all Japanese warriors as samurai and all samurai as warriors. As we have seen in the previous chapter, the samurai was a warrior class, but many of them also turned to the arts. And actually, that very term became widespread only as the civil war was slowly coming to an end and with the unification of Japan under the Tokugawa regime.

The most common term used to name warriors, in general, was bushi, literary translated as the men of the martial arts. It became prevalent in the Nara period in the 8ᵗʰ century, predating the word samurai for about 200 years. And when the word samurai was introduced, it was specifically used to distinguish warriors in service of the nobles. In the Kamakura period, samurai were the ones who were given an official rank by the shōgun or the imperial court. It was only in the later medieval period that this term indicated soldiers of a comparatively high social status. On the other hand, bushi always remained a term for warriors in general, but in later periods, they were all considered to be part of "warrior houses," or buke in Japanese. These grew from warrior bands, or bushidan, which served the nobles in the provinces, helping officials preserve peace and order. Over the centuries, buke became a word synonymous with bushi and began to refer to the entire warrior class. And warrior leaders, who commanded both the greatest armies and largest domains, grew ever more powerful during the Sengoku period, eventually becoming known as daimyō, meaning "great name." During that era, the warrior class became the pinnacle of Japanese society, if not in theory, then at least in practice.

It was in the era of daimyōs that the warfare in Japan became how most modern people envision it. During the classical era, wars were fought by the conscripted peasants who were led by nobles on the battlefield. But as the central government weakened, the conscription wavered. That left the nobles in need of armies who then had to pay for their services, actually creating the warrior class. But these were still relatively small armies, numbering in hundreds or at the utmost a few thousand people. And in that early medieval period, pretty much all of the people on battlefields were trained soldiers, and battles were more procedural. They were often fought by small armies in which individual soldiers broke off into one-on-one duels. In some cases, the battles were even decided by the duels of the two army generals themselves. But as the fighting grew fiercer and the stakes higher, and as Japan descended into the civil war, generals realized that relying on the warrior class wasn't enough. They once again started conscripting peasants for their armies, but now they were led by the trained samurai warriors, who were indeed the elite warriors of Japan. Armies grew larger, numbering up to 50,000 men, and they were better organized. Tactics also became more important as the battles became massive, no longer a matter of individual duels but of well-synchronized actions of thousands. And with that, the number of casualties grew as well, making the Sengoku period probably the bloodiest in Japanese history after World War II.

Sengoku period battle. Source: https://commons.wikimedia.org

However, despite the gritty reality of warfare in which the samurai showed little mercy to each other, they did have a philosophy and a code of conduct guiding them. Inspired by Chinese Confucian thoughts, some of the most important samurai ideals were loyalty and honor. It was a matter of personal and familial reputation, fulfilling one's duty toward both his superiors and inferiors. They were also expected to be well-mannered and dressed properly, as any imperfection would be seen as a sign of a personal character flaw. Another important part of the samurai life was marriage, as the Confucian patriarchal ideal saw it as a necessity for the harmony of society. If a samurai disobeyed the codes of conduct, he was expected to end his own life. It was done through a ritual called seppuku, or as it is also known harakiri. Committed by ripping open one's own stomach, seppuku was seen as a way to restore both personal and familial honor, as the abdomen was thought to be the residing place of the human soul. This ritual suicide was also done when ordered by the samurai's feudal lord when a warrior failed his task or duty. One step further was the practice of junshi. When a samurai lord performed seppuku or was killed in battle, in some occasions, he was followed in death by his own retainers as a sign of their loyalty.

Of course, these ideals weren't always followed, and there are many examples of disloyalty and cruelness among the samurai. But in later periods, the view on samurai became romanticized, and these virtues were the focus of their image. This was further strengthened under the Tokugawa regime when the set of rules for samurai were compiled. That guide for the Japanese warriors became known as bushido or the way of the warrior. It was also in that era that a romanticized image of the sword-wielding samurai became predominant. In reality, early samurais most commonly used bows and arrows which they usually fired while riding on horseback. Because of that, archery and horsemanship remained an important skill that the samurai trained in. They also used pole weapons like naginata, which was a wooden or metal pole with a curved single-edged blade on the end and looked like a combination of a sword and a spear. It was between 1.5 to 3 m (5 to 10 ft) long. Naginata was later replaced by yari, which was a plainer spear, 4.5 to 6.5 m (15 to 21 ft) long. Of course, most samurais wore swords, and not just one but usually two, a longer and a shorter one. But they were mostly used as a last resort or for dueling to settle personal differences out of combat.

Nonetheless, those swords were highly praised and seen as a class status symbol by the samurai. This is why by the late medieval period the craftsmanship of Japanese sword makers became astonishing. They became considerably adept in using folded and layered steel to create high-quality blades from fewer amounts of quality iron ore. This was done because Japan lacked the resources of iron and it had to be imported. This is how the samurai became known for their superior katana swords. But actually, the katana was just one type of sword they used, and it was among the last to develop, in the late 13th and early 14th centuries. It was about 60 cm (2 ft) long and suitable for dueling. On the other hand, tachi swords were older, dating back to the 10th century and were longer, approximately 90 cm (3 ft) long. And with the introduction of katanas, they were made more as regalia than as real combat weapons. Tantō and wakizashi were short swords or daggers, with the main differences being their length (tantōs were between 15 to 30 cm, or 6 to 12 in., and wakizashis were between 30 and 60 cm, or 12 to 24 in.) and that the tantō didn't have a handguard. All these types had their own varieties, but what they all had in common was that they were curved backward.

14th-century katana. Source: https://commons.wikimedia.org

Unlike European knights, the samurai didn't usually carry handheld shields. They did use mantlets, wooden barriers stuck in the ground that were used as protection from enemy projectiles. They also sometimes used a long piece of fabric draped over their backs so that it could catch arrows. This was the most effective during rapid maneuvers and charges that caused those pieces of fabric to billow up like a bag. It also proved useful for messengers who had no other way to defend themselves from their pursuers. But of course, the main type of defense was armor. The Japanese preferred lamellar armor, known as ō-yoroi, made from small leather or iron scales, often even combining the two to increase protection and decrease weight. They proved to be more effective and lighter than European chainmail of that era. In the late medieval period, a simplified version of ō-yoroi appeared, called haramaki. It was cheaper and often used for foot soldiers. At the same time, wealthier samurai were slowly starting to transition to dō, a type of plate armor which was necessitated by the arrival of firearms. Samurai also wore helmets, or kabuto, made out of sheets of iron or steel with flaps at the sides and back. That way they offered protection for the neck as well. Armors and helmets for the samurai had more than just a simple protective use. They were often colored and highly adorned with regalia and ornaments through which they showed their allegiances, inspired their fellow warriors, and instilled fear to the enemy. Together with swords, they were part of a family's heirlooms and often passed through generations of samurai families.

A Kamakura period armor and helmet
Source: https://commons.wikimedia.org

During the civil war, when armies grew in size, the samurai weren't alone on the battlefield anymore. They were in fact heavily outnumbered by common foot soldiers known as ashigaru (light of foot). These warriors usually lacked any complex military training and were supplied by their feudal lords. They wore simpler armors and conical helmets. Though they were usually made out of iron, sometimes they also wore leather equipment. The ashigaru were usually armed with pole weapons, usually yari and sometimes naginata, as they required less training to use proficiently. They were also used as archers, which to a degree diminished archery in the eyes of the samurai. By the end of the 16th century, some smaller numbers of ashigaru were armed with muskets as well, since firearms became more common on the battlefield. These troops were usually seen as less worthy and more replaceable than the samurai, who required years of harsh training to achieve their knowledge of both martial arts and strategy. Another type of combatant that appeared in medieval Japan was the sōhei or warrior monks. They started to appear in times of insecurity as a protection for the major Buddhist temples, and they proved to be formidable foes as they were both well-armed and skilled fighters. Despite being called monks, not all sōhei were part of the monastic order at the temples they served.

A warrior monk or sōhei. Source: https://commons.wikimedia.org

For that reason, it wasn't uncommon for sōhei to become a menace to society, robbing the commoners and expanding the lands belonging to the temples. Many imperial and shōgunal leaders fought hard against them. The last type of soldiers, if one can call them that, were the shinobi. To Westerners, they are more familiar as the ninja. In a romanticized view of the past, these were skilled acrobats, dressed in all black, climbing castle walls and assassinating their targets. They were the opposite of samurai ideals. However, the truth about them is much more mundane. Shinobi dressed to best suit with their surroundings, and their main task was espionage and sabotage, though they did sometimes assassinate people if needed. And they weren't the exact opposite of the valorous samurai, as they were hired and used by almost all daimyōs. By the very end of the medieval period, ninjutsu, the art of covert and guerrilla warfare, was slowly becoming integrated as a part of a samurai's training. The number of tools and weapons used by them is great, from katanas and throwing daggers and stars, to grappling hooks and smoke bombs. The secret to their success was adaptability. However, their usefulness was a short period, from the 14th to early 17th centuries, when Japan was in disarray. After that, the shinobi slowly died out.

That fate was shared by many other Japanese warriors after Tokugawa's victory. Many samurais were left without their masters, becoming ronin (floating men). Yet the militant spirit of the Japanese civilization endured. It was saved by the fact that the Tokugawa regime was still a shōgunate, a military government, which praised its roots and traditions, even though in later periods they presented that past in a very distorted and biased way. Thus, warriors remained an important part of the Japanese way of life even during their peacetime.

Chapter 8 – Religious Life in Japan

As in many other ancient societies, religion played an important role in the history of Japan. It was religion that shaped its art and culture, fostered connections with mainland Asia, and influenced the development of Japanese thought. Without religion, the Japanese civilization couldn't be understood, especially if we consider the fact that the emperor or tennō was first and foremost their religious leader and only secondly and sporadically their secular monarch. That connection comes from the indigenous religion of the Japanese known as Shinto.

Traditional Shinto temple. Source: https://commons.wikimedia.org

Literally translated it means "the way of the god," and it is based around worshiping a multitude of gods or deities known as kami. According to tradition, there are over eight million kami, and their nature is neutral. If worshipped properly, they are benevolent; if not, they turn destructive. This is why the ritual practices that include purifications, food offerings, dances, and festivals honoring the deities are central to Shinto. They are done to appease the kami. And central to it is the emperor, whose main religious task is to keep the entire country in favor of the gods. Another important aspect of kami worship is family and ancestors. Though there are Shinto temples, it isn't uncommon for families to have their own home shrines where they would pay respects to the deceased members of their families who would sometimes even be considered as kami themselves. These aspects show a strong Chinese influence on the Japanese religion, which predates the introduction of Buddhism. Shinto is also a very communal religion, which is exhibited through festivals and public rituals where all members of the community would pray for everyone's wellbeing. And as kami were also connected to nature itself, the ancient Japanese respected their surroundings, thinking that some of the deities were living in things like forests and rivers. The highest veneration of the natural world was reserved to the mountains which were thought to have the strongest connection both to the kami and their ancestors, which is why temples and shrines were often built on them.

What especially separates Shinto from most other religions in the world is the fact that it has no core sacred texts or founders. The traditions were "unified" and standardized only in the late medieval period with many local variations and customs. Yet there was a centralized state cult linked directly to the emperor and the imperial family. The tennō wasn't only a high priest, but through mythology, he was also a direct descendant of the creator gods that formed Japan. This is what kept the Yamato dynasty on the throne despite the fact that most of the later emperors held no real political power. Since the ancestors of their monarchs were gods, that meant that both the imperial family and their country were chosen and favored by the gods, making them impervious to outside attacks and superior to other civilizations. This notion was only heightened after the Mongol invasions in the 13th century.

Nevertheless, Shinto remained an open religion itself without disregarding other traditions or beliefs. This is why when Buddhism arrived there weren't any major turmoil or conflicts.

12ʰ-century Buddhist temple. Source: https://commons.wikimedia.org

On top of that, Buddhism itself isn't a very aggressive religion. Originating in India, it traveled through China to Japan. And since its arrival in the mid-6th century, it grew quickly, mostly thanks to the patronage of the early Yamato kings. The main Buddhist teachings of gaining enlightenment (nirvana) and liberation from suffering through meditation and morality of one's actions (karma) were rather compatible with Shinto. It is also important to point out that Buddhism had many different versions and teachings, both in Japan and the rest of Asia. So already by the classical Nara period, there were more than six different Buddhist schools in Japan, all preaching different paths toward nirvana. The first of those was founded by the Chinese Buddhist masters that migrated to Japan to spread their religion. Later on, new schools were founded by Japanese monks who went to China to gain sufficient knowledge and practice to create their own teachings. It was only in the late 12th and early 13th centuries that monks who were educated in Japan could attain the rank of a Buddhist master.

Though their ideas and teachings continued to be influenced by the religious developments in China, by that time, it became a common practice of the Buddhists in Japan to rely on temples and monks and established rituals to attain the enlightenment.

Zen master Dōgen. Source: https://commons.wikimedia.org

Yet for some monks, like famed Eisai Zenji and Dōgen Zenji, this approach was wrong. It was too reliant on others to achieve peace and nirvana, and it made people too dependent on monks. Those two separately traveled to China in the late 12th and early 13th centuries, bringing Zen Buddhism to Japan for the first time. First becoming Zen masters in Japan, they then preached that attaining nirvana could be realized through everyday life, by relying on oneself and more traditional practices such as meditation. This type of Buddhism was more monastic in its nature, and in the beginning, it wasn't as popular. However, the strict and hierarchical nature of Zen schools became more and more popular among the rising warrior class, and through the patronage of the Kamakura bakufu, the Hōjō family, and later on the Ashikaga shōgunate, it became the most influential Buddhist teachings. Its importance rose significantly when Zen monks started to participate in the shōgunal government from the 14ᵗʰ century onwards, as their temples became part of the state administrative system. The influence of Zen thought on Japanese culture became immense, from reintroducing the ideals of a moderate way of life to simpler things such as drinking tea.

That influence wasn't limited only to the Zen schools as Buddhism in general permeated Japanese art, their way of thinking, and civilization in general. And despite the supremacy achieved by Zen Buddhism, other schools never ceased to exist, and all of the temples continued to operate through the centuries, continuing and, in some cases, evolving their teachings and traditions. This coexistence was also eased by the fact that most of the Japanese continued to practice Shinto ceremonies, making their actual religion, in essence, a mixture of Shinto and Buddhist beliefs and customs. This was achievable as Buddhism never negated the existence of gods, and both religions had a close connection with the state as well as certain similar ideals. For example, both religions were focused on worldly problems like poverty and illness, while death was only a transition, not a permanent "end." And through Confucian influence, both Shinto and Buddhism saw the family as one of the sources of religious activity and respected their ancestors. And despite Zen teachings, most Buddhists and Shintoists relied on prayers, invocations, festivals, and ritual offerings to achieve their goals. Thus, despite never actually fusing into one religion, Buddhism and Shintoism remained inextricably linked. Even today most Japanese practice the syncretism of Buddhism and kami worship known as shinbutsu-shūgō.

However, there was one major difference between Shintoism and Buddhism. The latter was introduced by the Chinese, who brought literacy with them. As such, the earliest forms of education was tightly connected with Buddhist monks. In the classical period, education was only available to the nobles, who could afford to pay teachers, and those learning to become Buddhist priests. But as Buddhism started to gain wider popularity in the early middle ages, temples started opening schools for a broader population. However, literacy was in general still rather low and confined to aristocrats and the rising samurai class. In 1432, the Ashikaga School (Ashikaga Gakkō), which is originally thought to be founded in the ninth century, was restored, and it was connected with the ruling shōgunal family. And even though it was the first secular school, it was still headed by a Buddhist monk at the time of its creation. The curriculum was focused on military strategy and Confucian philosophy, as the students were supposed to be mainly from the warrior class. By the mid-16th century, this school had over 3,000 students from all over Japan. The education given in Ashikaga Gakko was of such quality that even the Jesuit missionary Francis Xavier expressed his admiration for it, which wasn't common for Christians to do for the population they were trying to convert.

Christianization of the Japanese in the 16th century was at best moderately successful. Missionaries, most commonly from the Jesuit and Franciscan order, were confronted by cultural differences and worldviews. The Japanese had a hard time accepting the idea that only those who accepted Christianity would be saved, meaning that their dead ancestors would be condemned for eternity no matter what. Despite that, it is estimated that by 1580 around 130,000 Japanese were converted in a population that numbered at least 8 to 10 million people. This number was heightened due to some of the converted feudal lords forcing their subjects to convert as well. The helping factor for the missionaries was the backing of Oda Nobunaga and Toyotomi Hideyoshi. They saw the opportunity to use Christians to oppose the mighty Buddhist temples which had grown too powerful to control, as well as to boost their economy by trading with the Europeans. But as unification was coming to a close, Christianity was seen as a threat to the unity and national identity of the Japanese. So, in 1587, Hideyoshi turned back on his stance toward them and ordered all missionaries to leave Japan. This order was enacted only sporadically, and Christian missionaries continued to work. When Tokugawa Ieyasu took control over Japan, he was tolerant toward the Christians to maintain friendly relations with the Western merchants. Yet later the Tokugawa bakufu started to shut off Japan from foreign influences, and governmental policies turned against the Christians. The shogunate officially banned Christianity in 1614 and issued another statement calling for the expulsion of all Christian missionaries. That same year, the shogunate began the systematic persecution of Christians. Buddhist temples were given the responsibility of verifying that a person, via the temple guarantee system (terauke seido), was not a Christian. By 1639, they had killed at least 1,000 Christians, expelled at least another 13,000 local Christians to Manila, and effectively ended the open practice of Christianity. It only survived by going underground.

For what has been said, it is obvious how important religion was for the history of Japan. Both Buddhism and Shintoism were close with the state, from ideological backgrounds to administration. And temples were crucial for spreading literacy, education, and knowledge in general. Not to mention that religious traditions were in part one of the many roots of the national identity of the Japanese. It bound both local and national communities through common practices and rituals and gave the Japanese their common mythical roots. And both Buddhism and Shintoism were, in fact, part of everyday life in ancient Japan, leaving an unquestionable mark on the evolution of its culture and civilization.

Chapter 9 – Japanese Culture

Like all other great civilizations, Japan created a unique culture. It was a mixture of indigenous traditions, Chinese and Buddhist influences, and, in later periods, warrior ideals. These combined together weaved a culture we know today, connecting various astonishing artworks and writings through the ages into one constantly growing and evolving yet still coherent system. And it is important to shed some light on that as well, as too many times when thinking about ancient Japan, we focus only on the wars and soldiers, intrigues and politics, and on generals and emperors. In fact, Japanese history is much more than just that.

Yamato-e style painting. Source: https://commons.wikimedia.org

One of the most recognizable forms of Japanese art is paintings. Developed with heavy Chinese influence, it can be divided into two major groups. The older group is the so-called kara-e (Chinese-style picture). First introduced in the Nara period, it drew its style directly from Chinese art. These are usually more monochromatic, using either just black and white or different shades of the same color. Another distinguishable detail is that the landscape is more mountainous, looking more like mainland

China than Japan. The other, younger group formed in the late Heian period and blossomed later in the medieval era, adding more vibrant and thicker colors while still representing the more gently rolling landscapes that characterize Japan. It is known as Yamato-e (Japanese-style picture). Of course, both of these styles evolved and changed over the years, influenced by historical developments. For example, Heian painters often focused on courtly themes, romances, and in general had more gentle themes. With the rise of the warrior class, painters turned toward representations of military conquests, war epics, and in general more masculine and martial types of art. By the 16ᵗʰ century, some painters also started depicting the everyday life of the different social classes. However, landscapes and religious themes remained a constant in ancient Japanese paintings. And unlike most European paintings, Japanese artists usually painted on silk or paper scrolls of various sizes, as well as wooden and paper doors and walls.

As such, paintings were used to decorate a wide array of places from private homes to palaces and courts as well as temples. In contrast to that, statues were usually found in temples. Most commonly made out of wood and in some cases bronze or clay, these sculptures customarily had Buddhist themes. The early sculptors from the Asuka period leaned toward unrealistic and mythical representations of their subjects with a feel of steadiness and godliness. Through the centuries, there was a slow shift toward a more human form grounded in realism. Sculptures were given a more dramatic feel with a more direct manifestation of emotions and movement. Despite that, serenity was still quite present. With the end of the Kamakura bakufu, realism was further enhanced to a measure where it became exaggerated realism. An example of that was the practice of using crystal insets for eyes (gyokugan, or "jewel eyes"). By the medieval era, it also became common to paint and decorate wooden sculptures, giving them a more vivid presence. In the earlier periods, sculptors were employed usually by temples themselves or in some cases the emperors, but in later medieval times, the patronage shifted toward the members of the higher warrior class. In that period, there is both a decline in the quality and quantity of statues, but also in some cases, those patrons also requested portrait statues of themselves, shifting slightly from the Buddhist themes.

12ᵗʰ-century wooden statue. Source: https://commons.wikimedia.org

Buddhism also influenced another more practical art form which is architecture. In the earliest periods, Japanese builders erected simple structures from unpainted and untreated wood with simple ornamentation. With the arrival of Buddhism, Chinese influence started to shift these characteristics toward colored and treated wood, with more decorations and higher and bigger structures. Tall multistory pagodas became the common type of building for Buddhist temples. But through time, Japanese architects realized that earthquakes were rather common in their country and employed the use of penetrating tie beams which gave structures more sturdiness and was also a simple way of decorating columns and beams. They also started using thicker woodwork which was more durable and imposing. And with the spreading of Zen ideas and the establishment of a militaristic society, in the middle ages, Japanese builders once again turned toward a more simplistic style of ornamentation. When Zen Buddhism arrived from China, it brought bell-shaped windows to Japanese architecture. By that time, pagodas were slowly going out of fashion. Zen principles also changed the gardens, introducing sand or gravel to replace water found in ponds and lakes, which were common in the earlier periods. In contrast to Buddhist architecture, Shinto shrines remained small and simple, usually built to resemble old granaries. The most recognizable aspect of Shinto architecture was the temple gate which, though simple in structure with two horizontal beams, played an important religious role as the gateway into the sacred precinct. Today that gate, known as torii, is accepted as a worldwide symbol of Shintoism.

Traditional Shinto torii gate. Source: https://commons.wikimedia.org

Both of these religions were also connected with other performing arts. Shinto priests performed kagura, the music and dance of the kami. It had various local variations, but it was at some point done by the emperor himself in the royal court. In

Buddhist rituals, it was common to use ritual chanting, dances, and various music. However, both music and dancing were common in non-religious forms. From the Nara period came the gagaku, musical tradition, and bugaku, dance tradition, which were performed at court. Despite being secular in nature, as these were connected with the court, they still had some religious connotations and as such were occasionally performed in both Shinto shrines and Buddhist temples. Like in other aspects of Japanese culture, the rise of the military class also affected the music. By the 12th century, recitals that told stories about battles and heroes accompanied by music became rather popular. Combining Buddhist chanting with court music, these were collectively known as heikyoku. These retellings of warrior tales were later expanded into reenactments by a small number of actors but still retained the form of a dramatic song and dance. These were known as kōwakamai and served as a precursor to the theater. Another form of a song influenced by the rise of the warrior class was the "banquet song," or enkyoku. As these were played at feasts and celebrations, they were less serious and a livelier version of music.

Late medieval musicians. Source: https://commons.wikimedia.org

Besides these, there were many variations of local or regional musical traditions and dances which historians collectively call folk music, yet not all of them are well known and studied. However, most of the music of ancient Japan was played on traditional instruments. The most common were the bamboo flute (shakuhachi), double reed flute (hichiriki) which sounds like the modern-day clarinet, 13-string zither-like instrument known as koto, a three-string plucked lute (shamisen), as well as kokyū, a bowed lute. It is clear that most of these were influenced by the Chinese tradition, though they were developed to suit the Japanese culture. The Japanese also had two different styles of drums. The large one is known as taiko, which is laid on the ground and beaten with thick sticks. The other style is called tsuzumi, which are handheld lacquered wooden drums in an hourglass shape. All of these instruments created various notes and rhythms, but in traditional Japanese music, silence (ma) or the space between the notes was also important. This was also seen in dances when performers paused between their movements. Such silences or pauses were seen as an integral part of the music while serving as a practical tool to heighten the audience's anticipation.

Dance and music evolved into theater which had two styles, noh and kyogen, and appeared in the late 14th and early 15th centuries. Both of these styles put an emphasis on mime and stylized dances and songs to retell a story, with a focus on human emotions. One of the characteristics of those types of acting was the use of certain established gestures and movements to signal to the audience about the actions and transitions that didn't actually happen onstage, like long travels. Noh was a serious dramatic form with plays retelling stories of gods and demons, and warriors and court ladies, and it was grounded in Buddhist sensibilities. In contrast to noh, kyogen was performed by amateurs who improvised comic reliefs acts, usually in between scenes or before a noh play. Thus, both styles often came in a package.

This early Japanese theater used both poems and prose, and they often told already known stories, many of them already told through literature. The earliest recorded stories were found in two chronicles *Kojiki* and *Nihon Shoki*. Written in the early 8ᵗʰ century, they combined both historical events and mythological tales. In that very same century, the first poems were recorded. Known as kanshi, they were written in the Chinese style with Chinese characters. By the Heian period, waka, or Japanese poems, having originated in the *Kojiki*, experienced a revival; these poems had aristocratic themes and values. Like all later poems, it also had a strict formulaic structure with a certain number of lines and syllables. In the middle ages, a new type of poem was created known as renga. It followed a similar pattern as waka, but it linked their verses into long stanzas. This allowed for more variety and led to the decline of waka in the 15ᵗʰ century. However, from shorter renga sections, a more internationally famous type of style arose, the haiku poem.

As for prose, it also developed in the medieval times, branching from chronicles into several other forms, with more warrior and worldly themes. One of the most widespread styles was the diary or memoir, which were recollections of certain events or travels. Similar to them were war tales (gunki monogatari). These narrated glorious battles, victories and defeats, and retold heroic feats. These reinforced warrior ethics and were very popular with the ruling warrior class of the medieval era. Essays, or zuihitsu (following the writing brush), were also written. These were diverse treatises or random thoughts, created from personal observations about nature and people and written with no specific structure in mind. It should be pointed out that literature was written almost exclusively by aristocrats and Buddhist monks. And among them, calligraphy was also popular. Introduced by the Chinese, in the early periods it was done with both Chinese characters (kanji) and style, but later many started using the Japanese writing system (kana) and developed an indigenous Japanese style. Calligraphy was rather popular in both the noble court as well as among the samurai. Warriors praised it as it required calmness, discipline, and precision, which is why it was also linked with Zen Buddhism in the medieval period.

In both calligraphy and other manners of writing, it was common to use both Chinese and Japanese characters. However, that doesn't mean that the Japanese were writing in the Chinese language. Instead, they used Chinese characters, or rather their pronunciation, to write down their own language in its own form and structure. That being said, it should be stressed that Chinese and Japanese languages, despite sounding similar to the untrained ear of the Westerner, have no common roots or connections. They are different languages. For this reason, the use of kanji was rather complicated, along with the added difficulty that it had two ways of pronunciation. This pushed Japanese scholars to develop kana, which was, in essence, a simplified version of the kanji characters with specifically designated syllable sounds linked with them. This made it much simpler to use for the Japanese. But throughout Japanese history, even today, both kana and kanji remain in use, both separately and in various combinations.

So far, most of the cultural achievements of ancient Japan were in various degrees influenced by the Chinese civilization, yet they were adopted and evolved into something that was more Japanese in its essence. Unfortunately, when it comes to natural sciences like medicine, mathematics, and astrology, the indigenous Japanese contributions were more than limited. In medicine, the traditional Chinese idea of a vital force known as qi (or ki in Japanese) was the main base of treatment. Thus, the focus was on the entire body and person, not singular symptoms. This was supplemented with the Buddhist ideas of karmic diseases from past lives. So, treatment was both spiritual and physical. The former was done through things like prayers or ritual cleansings, while the latter was done by using various plant and animal ointments, potions, creams, and similar concoctions. Japanese healers also practiced acupuncture as a way to unblock ki energy. Astronomy, another science, was used mostly for timekeeping and the calendar, which was based on the Chinese calendar and their astronomical practices and technologies. In mathematics, the Chinese system was in use throughout the ancient era; only after Tokugawa's unification did local mathematicians develop the Japanese mathematical system. Considering that the Japanese society was more military orientated, it isn't surprising that there weren't any considerable scientific breakthroughs in this era, but the Japanese did have a long tradition of making complex mechanisms, which is obvious from the rather quick adoption of firearms production. This can still be seen to this day as the Japanese are the leaders in robotics technology.

Similar to science, philosophy wasn't one of the important subjects to the ancient Japanese. The furthest extent was the adoption of Confucian ideals, as seen in the importance of propriety and retaining harmony with heaven. To the Japanese that meant it was important to act in a morally and socially acceptable manner, leading to a seemingly strict society. Another ideal of the Confucian teachings was the importance of family and familial piety, which heavily influenced the development of the clan system. However, this permeated the lower layers of society as well. In the basic family unit, or ie (house), the oldest man was the head of the household and held the highest responsibilities. But as idleness was frowned upon, everyone in the home was expected to do some work, regardless of age, gender, or even socioeconomic status. Women were tasked with maintaining the household while children were taught how to perform various housework usually early on in their life. Most of a child's education, especially for the lower classes, came from their parents. The actual houses in which they lived were usually small, simple, and adaptable structures, due to the volatile conditions of the climate and natural disasters. They were furnished in a simplistic manner with few pieces of furniture. They most commonly used tatami woven floor mats, zabuton cushions for sitting, short tables, and futon mattresses placed on the ground for sleeping. Heat and lighting typically came from a central fireplace.

That fireplace was also used for cooking. Traditional Japanese cuisine consisted of seafood, marine vegetation, seasonal vegetables, and rice, which constituted the bulk of the meal. The meat was seen as impure because of religious stipulations. So, the nobles and monks avoided it, while commoners and lower rank warriors consumed it more regularly. To supplement the lack of meat, soybean products were used. For example, they used miso, a nutritious grain and soybean paste made with rice or barley, and tofu. Common spices were soy sauce, ginger, wasabi (Japanese horseradish), and sansho, a powder made from ground seedpods of the prickly ash tree. During the medieval period, it was common for the nobles and higher classes to eat twice a day, while commoners, because of their more physically exhausting work, ate up to four times per day. Influenced by Chinese tradition, the Japanese consumed their meals with chopsticks, usually made from wood. One of the modern-day staples of Japanese cuisine is, of course, rice wine known as sake. Its roots can be found in the classical era, but it gained its popularity in the middle ages. This beverage was at first consumed at celebrations and festivals, and in later periods it became an everyday drink. It was also customary to drink tea after the meal. However, this tea was prepared and drank differently than in the famous tea ceremonies.

More art than anything else, these ceremonies of tea drinking were introduced with the arrival of Zen Buddhism, despite the fact that tea had been drunk in Japan since the 8th century. The ritual of preparing tea became known as chanoyu, meaning hot water for tea, or chado, the way of tea. It had very precise steps which were required to prepare a perfect sip of tea, as well as a dubious number of specialized utensils used in its preparations. Because of this, mastering the ceremony took years of practice and gathering of different tools. These ceremonies were usually reserved for the upper class. However, drinking tea in such a manner wasn't just showing off one's knowledge and discipline. It also had a more spiritual role. Shinto and Buddhist ideals were connected with it, as it reflected harmony and calmness. For that reason, tea practitioners do not prefer to define their gatherings as "ceremonies" because that word implies a stiffness that they try to eliminate through their meditative and religious concepts of tea preparation.

Modern Japanese tea ceremony. Source: https://commons.wikimedia.org

Despite that, the ancient Japanese culture embodied strictness and stiff rules which can also be seen through the hairstyles worn. They reflected one's age, status, and sexuality. For example, samurais wore their hair in a topknot which was, at the start, a pragmatic need of a warrior as loose hair could be pulled in battle. Later on, it started to represent belonging to a warrior class in general. Up to the 16th century, women kept their hair long and straight. Afterward, they slowly began to put their hair up and decorate them with various combs, pins, and other ornaments. Cosmetics were used by both men and women on a regular basis. Pale skin was seen as the most desirable, so many women used face powder known as oshiroi to whiten their faces. And contrary to present-day standards, blackened teeth were a common trend. It was done by an oxidized liquid which also preserved the teeth. This practice was called ohaguro, and it was used mostly by women, though in the late medieval period, it became popular among men as well. The clothing they wore was also indicative of one's class and profession. For example, in the Kamakura period, the typical warrior uniform consisted of a hunting jacket (kariginu) and a cloak (suikan). Formal attire worn by women included a robe (uchiki), skirt-trousers (hakama), and a silk garment with short sleeves (kosode). As for the kimono, the most famous part of traditional Japanese clothing, it became popular in the Nara period and remains in use to this day.

Clothes varied in material, with silk and cotton being used by the higher classes. They were usually rather colorful, and traditionally, they covered as much skin as possible. It was regarded that the less skin seen, the higher status of the person wearing the clothes. And these clothes are actually a good metaphor for the ancient Japanese culture in general. It was strict, had certain rules, and it varied between classes. It looks a bit tight and restraining, but it is also very beautiful and full of color and uniqueness. And in every aspect, one can see both indigenous roots and foreign influences. This is what makes Japanese culture, even today, unique, as it is a mix of both old and new, of domestic and native. And those characteristics we can track all the way back to the classical period of Japanese history when the foundations of the Japanese civilization were laid.

Conclusion

Ancient Japan went through various changes through history, from a unified courtly and art-loving country to a militaristic, pragmatic, and divided society. It saw the rise and fall of emperors, nobility, and shōguns in an ever-changing political landscape. Yet it would be wrong to focus solely on the wars and intrigues. Ancient Japanese society left a substantial cultural heritage that became an important part of the world's civilizations. And because of its uniqueness, even today it captivates people's imagination, especially after Japan's economic and cultural renaissance of the late 20th century when its culture became globally recognizable. Looking at it today, we can see traces of old traditions and roots of this great civilization that span almost 2,000 years.

When looking at both Japanese history and its culture, it becomes obvious that it is a civilization of paradoxes and opposites. However, its most striking characteristic, what makes it so unique, is its relations to other civilizations. Be it through pure luck or some higher reasoning, the Japanese throughout the past knew when it was time to open their borders and learn from their surroundings and when it was a good time to close them down and develop their own traditions, building on the influences of others. And they kept doing so even after the ancient times. When the Tokugawa regime solidified its rule, Japan closed its borders in the face of the Western colonizers, saving their country both from exploitation and their culture from being overwhelmed. But in the mid-19th century, when Japan saw that it was falling behind the rest of the world, it reopened its borders. Through the Meiji restoration, it learned from others around the world to create a modern and successful country once again before closing itself from foreign influences in the early 20th century, feeling that the old Japanese traditions were in danger of being forgotten. This ultimately led to the notorious crimes during World War II; however, the Japanese learned from that as well. They realized that the best path is a mixture of sticking to one's own tradition but also leaving a door open for new things to come from outside.

It is exactly that mixture of indigenous traditions, thoughts, and ideas mixed with foreign influences that makes Japanese culture so fascinatingly unique. It is what makes this civilization captivating today, and it is a lesson that every civilization, every nation, every society, and every person today should remember. The road to success is paved with accepting new and mixing it with the old, accepting the unfamiliar and exotic while keeping the local customs alive. This is one of the lessons that history can teach us because it connects the past with the present while keeping an eye on the future. This is why it is important to learn about the past of not only our own cultures and countries but from nations all across the world. Understanding others better will help us better understand ourselves. And that makes us capable of accepting both our own traditions as well as of those that come from different cultures, leading to a healthier world society and a greater future.

Bibliography

Chey O.S., *China Condensed: 5000 Years of History and Culture*, Marshall Cavendish Editions 2008.

Clunas Craig, *Art in China*, Oxford University Press 1997.

Dawei C. and Yanjing S., *China's History*, Cengage Learning 2011.

Ebrey Patricia B., *Chinese Civilization: A Sourcebook*, The free press 1993.

Fairbank J.F. and Goldman M., *China: A New History*, Harvard university press 2006.

Gernet Jacques, *A History of Chinese Civilization*, Cambridge University Press 1996.

Giles H.A., *Religions of Ancient China*, Blackmask Online 2000.

Greenberger Robert, *The Technology of Ancient China*. Rosen Publishing Group 2006.

Hinsch, Bret, *Women in Imperial China*, Rowman & Littlefield Publishers 2002.

Keay John, *China: A History*, Harper Press 2009.

Keightley D.N., *Origins of Chinese Civilization*, University of California press 1993.

Kinney A.B. and Hardy G., *The Establishment of the Han Empire and Imperial China*, Greenwood Press 2005.

Loewe M. and Shaughnessy E.L., *The Cambridge History of Ancient China*, Cambridge University Press 1999.

Morton W.S. and Lewis C.M., *China: Its History and Culture*, McGraw-Hill 2005.

Pletcher Kenneth, *The History of China*, Britannica Educational Publishing 2011.

Twitchett D. and Fairbank J.F., *The Cambridge History of China: Vol. 1*, Cambridge University Press 1986.

Watson W., *The Arts of China to AD 1900*, Yale University Press 1995.

Xueqin L., *Eastern Zhou and Qin Civilizations*, Yale University Press 1985.

Andressen, Curtis A., A Short History of Japan: From Samurai to Sony, Allen & Unwin 2002.

Henshall, Kenneth G., *A History of Japan: From Stone Age to Superpower*, Palgrave Macmillan 2004.

Beasley, W. G., *The Japanese Experience: A Short History of Japan*, Weidenfeld & Nicolson 1999.

Kozo Yamamura, *The Cambridge History of Japan: Vol. 3 Medieval Japan*, Cambridge University Press 1990.

John Whitney Hall, *The Cambridge History of Japan: Vol. 4 Early Modern Japan*, Cambridge University Press 1991.

Delmer M. Brown, *The Cambridge History of Japan: Vol. 1 Ancient Japan*, Cambridge University Press 1993.

Donald Shively and William H. McCullough, *The Cambridge History of Japan: Vol. 2 Heian Japan*, Cambridge University Press 1999.

John A. Ferejohn and Frances McCall Rosenbluth, *War and State Building in Medieval Japan*, Stanford University Press 2010.

Friday, Karl F., *Samurai, Warfare & the State in Early Medieval Japan*, Routledge 2004.

Deal, William E., *Handbook to Life in Medieval and Early Modern Japan*, Facts on File 2006.

Oyler, Elizabeth, *Swords, Oaths, and Prophetic Visions: Authoring Warrior Rule in Medieval Japan*, University of Hawai'i Press 2006.

Stephen Trunbull, *Warriors of Medieval Japan*, Osprey Publishing 2005.

Anthony J. Bryant, *The Samurai*, Osprey Publishing 1989.

Check out another book by Captivating History

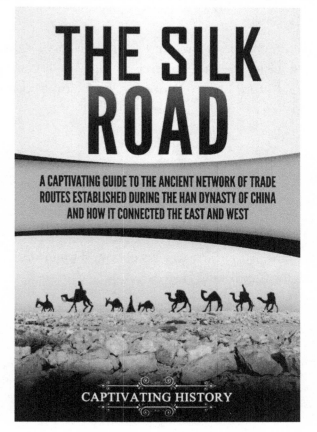

Free Bonus from Captivating History (Available for a Limited time)

Hi History Lovers!

Now you have a chance to join our exclusive history list so you can get your first history ebook for free as well as discounts and a potential to get more history books for free! Simply visit the link below to join.

Captivatinghistory.com/ebook

Also, make sure to follow us on Facebook, Twitter and Youtube by searching for Captivating History.

Made in the USA
Coppell, TX
28 June 2020

29711456R00146